THEY FIGHT
Classical to Contemporary
Stage Fight Scenes

They Fight

Classical to Contemporary Stage Fight Scenes

Edited by Kyna Hamill
with Don Weingust

CAREER DEVELOPMENT SERIES

A Smith and Kraus Book

Published by Smith and Kraus, Inc.
177 Lyme Road, Hanover, NH 03755
www.SmithKraus.com

First Edition: April 2003
10 9 8 7 6 5 4 3 2 1
Manufactured in the United States of America

Cover art by Lisa Goldfinger
Text design by Julia Hill Gignoux, Freedom Hill Design

Library of Congress Cataloging-in-Publication Data
They fight : classical to contemporary stage fight scenes /
edited by Kyna Hamill. —1st ed.
p. cm. — (Career development series)
ISBN 1-57525-322-4
1. Stage fighting. 2. Drama. I. Hamill, Kyna. II. Series.
PN2071.F54 2003
808.82—dc21   2003041505

Thanks

I would like to thank Don Weingust for his work on the Shakespeare scenes. I am grateful to Laurence Senelick and Tom Connolly for their comments and suggestions regarding this undertaking and for unknowingly leading me toward some of these plays during my courses with them. A special thanks to Anthony Cornish and the students in the "Weapons and Words" class at Tufts (Spring 2001), who performed several of these scenes in class and showed me that they worked in performance. Much esteem goes out to J.P. Fournier, a great teacher of mine and kind advocate of this project.

— Kyna Hamill

❖ ❖ ❖

This book is dedicated to Lukasz for his patience and help and for always being a strong supporter of all my endeavors.

Contents

Scenes for Groups of Three or More

* Can be played in pairs if adjusted.

Foreword

This book developed out of my own experience as a student of stage combat. In examinations and workshops, I noticed that many scenes were being performed over and over, and in some cases, dialogue was being invented on the spot — which may have served its purpose for the exam, but allowed for no character development for the actor. For performers of violence on the stage, there is a lot more than just fight technique and safety that needs to be considered. There is a reason for all this violence, whether it is comical or brutal. Why do so many characters resort to violence to solve their difficulties? Why is violence so commonly portrayed on stage? I have heard one teacher eloquently say that violence occurs when the words run out. Violence must come from somewhere, and actors who are looking to develop their fight skills should consider the very important moments building up to the fight and, of course, the consequences of such actions.

There have always been scenes from which to work (otherwise why would we be doing what we do!), but they have never been put together and made easily available to students and teachers. I have read a lot of plays, well known to stage fighters and some perhaps new. My intention is to open up the repertoire of scenes from which to work and to uncover some new plays for production by students and directors of stage fighting.

I have another agenda in this collection. As a woman in the field, I understand the difficulty of not only proving myself a worthy opponent but also in finding scenes where I could be proactive in the fight. I think I have found some interesting scenes for women to play, some in the usual victim roles and some so feisty that they will leave our opponents wondering what happened!

I have tried to choose moments that set up the fight and give some idea of what might happen after the violence has taken place. This is by no means a stage-fight manual; there are other worthy resources to look to in developing your fight skills. I have suggested possible weapons according to the context and period of the scene, but I urge readers to be creative in choosing weapons and developing choreography. The point of this book is to be a resource, not an authoritative listing of how each fight should be performed.

I hope this book will be valuable for actors, teachers, and directors in the study of fighting for the stage. Most of these plays are readily available to be studied — as they should be — beyond the scenes that are included here. The more obscure plays that are included can, with some time, be found in old anthologies, or on microfiche. This collection spans both time and location, and it says much about the culture from which each play was developed. Violence is by no means a phenomenon of the twentieth and twenty-first centuries. We can see in this book that the performance of violence on stage, with the exception of a few periods, has and will continue to reflect the manifestation of violence in our culture be it justified, or not.

Kyna Hamill
Medford, Massachusetts
July 2002

Scenes for Two Men

❖ ❖ ❖

Orlando Furioso
by Robert Greene (1594)

ORLANDO
ORGALIO: his page

> Orlando, a descendent of the Royal House of France, has
> been banished to Africa by his uncle Charlemagne. The
> King of Africa's daughter, Angelica, has chosen Orlando to
> be her husband and heir to the throne, but Sacripant, jeal-
> ous of her choice, has framed her to make it look like she
> is having an affair with Orlando's friend, Medor. Believing
> her infidelity to be true, the King banishes Angelica, and
> Orlando, thinking she is dead, goes insane. Here, Orlando
> comes upon his page and raves at the loss of Angelica.

> Suggested weapon: stick

> *Enter Orlando attired like a madman.*

ORLANDO: Woods, trees, leaves; leaves, trees, woods; *Tria se-
quuntur tria.* — Ho, Minerva! salve, good morrow; how
do you do today? Tell me sweet goddess, will Jove send
Mercury to Calypso, to let me go? Will he? Why, then, he's
a gentleman, every hair o' the head on him. — But, ho, Or-
galio! Where art thou, boy?
(Enter Orgalio.)
ORGALIO: Here, my lord; did you call me?
ORLANDO: No, nor name thee.
ORGALIO: Then God be with you.
(Goes to leave.)
ORLANDO: Nay, prithee, Good Orgalio, stay; canst though not
tell me what to say?
ORGALIO: No, by my troth.

ORLANDO: O, this it is; Angelica is dead.

ORGALIO: Why, then, she shall be buried.

ORLANDO: But my Angelica is dead.

ORGALIO: Why, it may be so.

ORLANDO: But she's dead and buried.

ORGALIO: Ay, I think so.

ORLANDO: Nothing but "I think so," and "It may be so"!
   (He beats him.)

ORGALIO: What do you mean, my lord?

ORLANDO: Why, shall I tell you that my love is dead,
   And can ye not weep for her?

ORGALIO: Yes, yes, my lord, I will.

ORLANDO: Well, do so, then. Orgalio.

ORGALIO: My lord?

ORLANDO: Angelica is dead. *(Orgalio cries.)* Ah, poor slave!
   So, cry no more now.

ORGALIO: Nay, I have quickly done.

ORLANDO: Orgalio.

ORGALIO: My lord?

ORLANDO: Medor's Angelica is dead.
   (Orgalio cries, and Orlando beats him again.)

ORGALIO: Why do you beat me, my lord?

ORLANDO: Why, slave, wilt thou weep for Medor's Angelica?
   Thou must laugh for her.

ORGALIO: Laugh! Yes, I'll laugh all day and you will.

ORLANDO: Orgalio.

ORGALIO: My lord?

ORLANDO: Medor's Angelica is dead.

ORGALIO: Ha, ha, ha, ha!

ORLANDO: So, 'tis well now.

ORGALIO: Nay, this is easier than the other was.

ORLANDO: Now away! Seek the herb moly; for I must to hell,
   To seek for Medor and Angelica.

ORGALIO: I know not the herb moly, i' faith.

ORLANDO: Come, I'll lead ye to it by the ears.

ORGALIO: 'Tis here, my lord, 'tis here.

ORLANDO: 'Tis indeed. Now to Charon, bid him dress his boat,

ORGALIO: For he had never such a passenger.

ORLANDO: Shall I tell him your name?

ORLANDO: No, then he will be afraid, and not be at home.

(Exit Orgalio.)

❖ ❖ ❖

The Tragedy of Macbeth
by William Shakespeare (c. 1605-1606)
edited by Don Weingust

MACBETH: King of Scotland
MACDUFF

Having killed King Duncan to assume his throne, Macbeth interprets as suggestions of invulnerability the twin prophecies that he "shall never vanquish'd be, until / Great Birnam Wood, to high Dunsinane Hill / Shall come against him" and "none of woman born / shall harm" him. Macbeth briefly contemplates taking his own life in the "Roman" fashion as he despairs over the death of his wife and the apparent fruition of one of the prophecies: Duncan's son Malcolm has led an army, camouflaged by tree limbs cut from Birnam Wood, against his fortress at Dunsinane. A vengeful Macduff, whose wife and children were murdered on Macbeth's orders, reveals that he had not been born naturally but was "untimely ripped" from his mother's womb. Macduff engages Macbeth in mortal combat.

Suggested weapons: broadswords, gauntlet

Enter Macbeth.

MACBETH: Why should I play the Roman Fool, and die
On mine own sword? whiles I see lives, the gashes
Do better upon them.
(Enter Macduff.)
MACDUFF: Turn Hell-hound, turn!
MACBETH: Of all men else I have avoided thee:
But get thee back, my soul is too much charg'd
With blood of thine already.
MACDUFF: I have no words,
My voice is in my Sword, thou bloodier Villain

Than terms can give thee out.
(They fight. An alarum sounds.)

MACBETH: Thou loosest labor

As easy may'st thou the intrenchant Air
With thy keen Sword impress, as make me bleed:
Let fall thy blade on vulnerable Crests,
I bear a charmed Life, which must not yield
To one of woman born.

MACDUFF: Despair thy Charm,

And let the Angel whom thou still hast serv'd
Tell thee, Macduff was from his Mother's womb
Untimely ripp'd.

MACBETH: Accursed be that tongue that tells me so;

For it hath Cow'd my better part of man:
And be these Juggling Fiends no more believ'd,
That palter with us in a double sense,
That keep the word of promise to our ear,
And break it to our hope. I'll not fight with thee.

MACDUFF: Then yield thee Coward,

And live to be the show, and gaze o'th' time.
We'll have thee, as our rarer Monsters are
Painted upon a pole, and under-writ,
"Here may you see the Tyrant."

MACBETH: I will not yield

To kiss the ground before young Malcolm's feet,
And to be baited with the Rabble's curse.
Though Birnam wood be come to Dunsinane,
And thou oppos'd, being of no woman born,
Yet I will try the last. Before my body,
I throw my warlike Shield: Lay on Macduff,
And damn'd be him, that first cries hold, enough.
(Exeunt fighting. Alarums.)
(Enter fighting, Macbeth is slain.)

❖ ❖ ❖

Women Beware Women
by Thomas Middleton (c. 1613–1614)

HIPPOLITO: brother to Livia
LEANTIO: a commercial agent, husband to Bianca
PAGE

> The Duke has told Hippolito that he has found a suitor for
> his widowed sister, Livia, and reveals that she has been se-
> cretly having an affair with Leantio, who is already mar-
> ried. Seeking to defend his sister's reputation, and appease
> the Duke's choice for her, Hippolito seeks out Leantio to
> fight.

Suggested weapons: rapiers

Florence. Enter Hippolito.

HIPPOLITO: The morning so far wasted, yet his baseness
    So impudent? See if the very sun do not blush at him!
    Dare he do thus much, and know me alive!
    Put case one must be vicious, as I know myself
    Monstrously guilty, there's a blind time made for't;
    He might use only that, 'twere conscionable.
    Art, silence, closeness, subtlety, and darkness
    Are fit for such a business. But there's no pity
    To be bestowed on an apparent sinner,
    An impudent daylight lecher! The great zeal
    I bear to her advancement in this match
    With Lord Vincentio, as the Duke has wrought it,
    To the perpetual honour of our house,
    Puts fire into my blood, to purge the air
    Of this corruption, fear it spread too far,
    And poison the whole hopes of this fair fortune.

I love her good so dearly, that no brother
Shall venture farther for a sister's glory
Than I for her preferment.
(Enter Leantio and a Page.)
LEANTIO: Once again
I'll see that glist'ring whore shines like a serpent,
Now the court sun's upon her. Page!
PAGE: Anon, sir!
LEANTIO: I'll go in state too; see the coach be ready.
(Exit Page.)
I'll hurry away presently.
HIPPOLITO: Yes, you shall hurry,
And the devil after you; take that at setting forth!
(Strikes Leantio.)
Now, and you'll draw, we are upon equal terms, sir.
Thou took'st advantage of my name in honour
Upon my sister; I nev'r saw the stroke
Come, till I found my reputation bleeding;
And therefore count it I no sin to valour
To serve thy lust so. Now we are of even hand,
Take your best course against me. You must die.
LEANTIO: How close sticks envy to man's happiness!
When I was poor and little cared for life,
I had no such means offered me to die,
No man's wrath minded me. *(Draws his sword.)*
Slave, I turn this to thee,
To call thee to account for a wound lately
Of a base stamp upon me.
HIPPOLITO: 'Twas most fit
For a base mettle. Come and fetch one now
More noble, then, for I will use thee fairer
Man thou hast done thine own soul or our honour;
And there I think 'tis for thee.
(They fight and Leantio falls.)

VOICE: *(Within.)* Help, help, oh part 'em!

LEANTIO: False wife! I feel now th'hast prayed heartily for me.
Rise, strumpet, by my fall, thy lust may reign now;
My heart-string and the marriage-knot that tied thee
Breaks both together. *(Dies.)*

HIPPOLITO: There I heard the sound on't,
And never liked string better.

❖ ❖ ❖

The Devil's Law-Case
by John Webster (c. 1617)

CONTARINO: a nobleman in love with Jolenta
ERCOLE: a Knight of Malta also in love with Jolenta

> After selling a piece of land to Romelio, Contarino, a nobleman, makes it clear that he would like to marry Romelio's sister, Jolenta. Romelio assures Contarino that his widowed mother will agree; however, she has designs on Contarino and promises Jolenta to Ercole, a Knight of Malta, also of good fortune. Jolenta, brokenhearted at being forced to marry Ercole, sleeps with Contarino in the hopes that a lawyer will wed them before she must marry Ercole. Contarino nobly challenges Ercole to a duel to decide who will have her.

> Suggested weapons: rapiers, gauntlet

> *Naples. Enter Ercole, Contarino.*

CONTARINO: Sir, my love to you has proclaimed you one,
　　Whose word was still led by noble thought,
　　And that thought followed by as fair a deed.
　　Deceive not that opinion; we were students
　　At Padua together, and have long
　　To th' world's eye shown like friends.
　　Was it hearty on your part to me?
ERCOLE: Unfeigned.
CONTARINO: You are false
　　To the good thought I held of you, and now
　　Join the worst part of man to you, your malice,
　　To uphold that falsehood; sacred innocence
　　Is fled your bosom. Signor, I must tell you,
　　To draw the picture of unkindness truly

Is to express two that have dearly loved,
And fall'n at variance. 'Tis a wonder to me,
Knowing my interest in the fair Jolenta,
That you should love her.

ERCOLE: Compare her beauty and my youth together,
And you will find the fair effects of love
No miracle at all.

CONTARINO: Yes, it will prove
Prodigious to you. I must stay your voyage.

ERCOLE: Your warrant must be mighty.

CONTARINO: It's a seal
From heaven to do it, since you would ravish from me
What's there entitled mine. And yet I vow,
By the essential front of spotless virtue,
I have compassion of both our youths;
To approve which, I have not ta'en the way,
Like an Italian, to cut your throat
By practice, that had given you now for dead,
And never frowned upon you.

ERCOLE: You deal fair, sir.

CONTARINO: Quit me of one doubt, pray, sir.

ERCOLE: Move it.

CONTARINO: 'Tis this:
Whether her brother were a main instrument
In her design for marriage.

ERCOLE: If I tell truth,
You will not credit me.

CONTARINO: Why?

ERCOLE: I will tell you truth,
Yet show some reason you have not to believe me.
Her brother had no hand in't: is't not hard
For you to credit this? For you may think
I count it baseness to engage another
Into my quarrel, and for that take leave
To dissemble the truth. Sir, if you will fight
With any but myself, fight with her mother:

She was the motive.

CONTARINO: I have no enemy in the world then, but yourself;
　　You must fight with me.

ERCOLE: I will, sir.

CONTARINO: And instantly.

ERCOLE: I will haste before you; point whither.

CONTARINO: Why, you speak nobly; and for this fair dealing,
　　Were the rich jewel which we vary for
　　A thing to be divided, by my life,
　　I would be well content to give you half;
　　But since 'tis vain to think we can be friends,
　　'Tis needful one of us be ta'en away
　　From being the other's enemy.

ERCOLE: Yet methinks.
　　This looks not like a quarrel.

CONTARINO: Not a quarrel?

ERCOLE: You have not apparelled your fury well;
　　It goes too plain, like a scholar.

CONTARINO: It is an ornament
　　Makes it more terrible; and you shall find it
　　A weighty injury and attended on
　　By discreet valour, because I do not strike you,
　　Or give you the lie; such foul preparatives
　　Would show like the stale injury of wine.
　　I reserve my rage to sit on my sword's point,
　　Which a great quantity of your best blood
　　Cannot satisfy.

ERCOLE: You promise well to yourself.
　　Shall's have no seconds?

CONTARINO: None for fear of prevention.

ERCOLE: The length of our weapons?

CONTARINO: We'll fit them by the way.
　　So, whether our time calls us to live or die,
　　Let us do both like noble gentlemen,
　　And true Italians.

ERCOLE: For that let me embrace you.

(They embrace.)

CONTARINO: Methinks, being an Italian, I trust you
　　To come somewhat too near me;
　　But your jealousy gave that embrace to try
　　If I were armèd, did it not?

ERCOLE: No, believe me.
　　I take your heart to be sufficient proof,
　　Without a privy coat; and for my part,
　　A taffeta is all the shirt of mail
　　I am armed with.

CONTARINO: You deal equally.
　　(Both exit. Time passes: four days.)
　　(Re-enter Ercole and Contarino.)

CONTARINO: You'll not forgo your interest in my mistress?

ERCOLE: My sword shall answer that. Come, are you ready?

CONTARINO: Before you fight, sir, think upon your cause,
　　It is a wondrous foul one, and I wish
　　That all your exercise these four days past
　　Had been employed in a most fervent prayer,
　　And the foul sin for which you are to fight
　　Chiefly remembered in't.

ERCOLE: I'd as soon take
　　Your counsel in divinity at this present,
　　As I would take a kind direction from you
　　For the managing my weapon; and indeed,
　　Both would show much alike.
　　Come, are you ready?

CONTARINO: Bethink yourself
　　How fair the object is that we contend for.

ERCOLE: O, I cannot forget it.
　　(They fight and Contarino wounds Ercole.)

CONTARINO: You are hurt.

ERCOLE: Did you come hither only to tell me so,
　　Or to do it? I mean well, but 'twill not thrive.

CONTARINO: Your cause, your cause, sir:
　　Will you yet be a man of conscience, and make

Restitution for your rage upon your deathbed?

ERCOLE: Never, till the grave gather one of us.

(They fight and Contarino wounds Ercole again.)

CONTARINO: That was fair, and home, I think.

ERCOLE: You prate as if you were in a fence-school.

CONTARINO: Spare your youth, have compassion on yourself.

ERCOLE: When I am all in pieces! I am now unfit
For any lady's bed; take the rest with you.

(Contarino, wounded, falls upon Ercole.)

CONTARINO: I am lost in too much daring: yield your sword.

ERCOLE: To the pangs of death I shall, but not to thee.

CONTARINO: You are now at my repairing, or confusion:
Beg your life.

ERCOLE: O most foolishly demanded,
To bid me beg that which thou canst not give.

(Ercole loses consciousness.)

❖ ❖ ❖

The Unnatural Combat
by Phillip Massinger (c. 1624-1625)

MALEFORT SENIOR: admiral of Marseilles
MALEFORT JUNIOR: his son

The admiral of Marseilles, Malefort Sr., is being tried for offenses against the navy, including keeping the plunder from pirates for himself and selling the sailors for slaves. During his trial, he claims that he has been mistaken with his son, Malefort Jr., who has taken up with the pirates. A sea Captain arrives on behalf of Malefort Jr., seeking to organize a duel between him and his father, citing a charge to be revealed when they meet. Malefort Sr. agrees, and we learn from his son that his father really is responsible for the charges and will shamelessly take his son's life to keep the truth from ever being known.

Suggested weapons: rapier, case of rapiers

Marseilles, an open space without the city.

MALEFORT SENIOR: Now we are alone sir;
    And thou hast liberty to unload the burthen
    Which thou groan'st under. Speak thy griefs.
MALEFORT JUNIOR: I shall, sir;
    But in a perplex'd form and method, which
    You only can interpret: Would you had not
    A guilty knowledge in your bosom, of
    The language which you force me to deliver,
    So I were nothing! As you are my father,
    I bend my knee, and, uncompell'ed, profess
    My life, and all that's mine, to be your gift;
    And that in a son's duty I stand bound
    To lay this head beneath your feet, and run

All desperate hazards for your ease and safety:
But this confest on my part, I rise up,
And not as with a father, (all respect
Love, fear and reverence cast off,) but as
A wicked man, I thus expostulate with you.
Why have you done that which I dare not speak,
And in the action changed the humble shape
Of my obedience, to rebellious rage,
And insolent pride? And with shut eyes constrain'd me
To run my bark of honour on a shelf
I must not see, nor, if I saw it, shun it?
In my wrongs nature suffers, and looks backward,
And mankind trembles to see me pursue
What beasts would fly from. For when I advance
This sword, as I must do, against your head,
Piety will weep, and filial duty mourn,
To see their altars which you built up in me,
In a moment razed and ruin'd. That you could
(From my grieved soul I wish it.) but produce,
To qualify, not excuse, your deed of horror,
One seeming reason, that I might fix here,
And move no further!

MALEFORT SENIOR: Have I so far lost
A father's power, that I must give account
Of my actions to my son? Or must I plead
As a fearful prisoner at the bar, while he
That owes his being to me sits a judge
To censure that, which only by myself
Ought to be question'd? Mountains sooner fall
Beneath their valleys, and the lofty pine
Pay homage to the bramble, or what else is
Preposterous in nature, ere my tongue
In one short syllable yield satisfaction
To any doubt of thine; nay, though it were
A certainty disdaining argument!
Since, though my deeds wore hell's black livery,

To thee they should appear triumphal robes,
Set off with glorious honour, thou being bound
To see with my eyes, and to hold that reason,
That takes or birth or fashion from my will.

MALEFORT JUNIOR: This sword divides that slavish knot.

MALEFORT SENIOR: It cannot:
It cannot, wretch; and if thou but remember
From whom thou hadst this spirit, thou dar'st not hope it.
Who trained thee up in arms but I? Who taught thee
Men were men only when they durst look down
With scorn on death and danger, and condemn'd
All opposition, till plumed Victory
Had made her constant stand upon their helmets?
Under my shield thou hast fought as securely
As the young eaglet, cover'd with the wings
Of her fierce dam, learns how and where to prey.
All that is manly in thee, I call mine;
But what is weak and womanish, thine own.
And what I gave, since thou art proud, ungrateful,
Presuming to contend with him, to whom
Submission is due, I will take from thee.
Look, therefore, for extremities, and expect not
I will correct thee as a son, but kill thee
As a serpent swollen with poison; who surviving
A little longer, with infectious breath,
Would render all things near him, like itself,
Contagious. Nay, now my anger's up,
Ten thousand virgins kneeling at my feet,
And with one general cry howling for mercy,
Shall not redeem thee.

MALEFORT JUNIOR: Thou incensed Power,
Awhile forbear thy thunder! Let me have
No aid in my revenge, if from the grave
My mother —

MALEFORT SENIOR: Thou shalt never name her more.
    (They fight. Young Malefort is slain.)

Were a new life hid in each mangled limb,
I would search and find it; and howe'er to some
I may seem cruel thus to tyrannize
Upon this senseless flesh, I glory in it. —
That I have the power to be unnatural,
Is my security; die all my fears,
And walking jealousies, which have so long
Been my tormentors! There's now no suspicion:
A fact, which I alone am conscious of,
Can never be discover'd, or the cause
That call'd this duel on, I being above
All perturbations; nor is it in
The power of fate, again to make me wretched.

❖ ❖ ❖

The Tragical History of King Richard III
by Colly Cibber (1700)

RICHARD: King of England
RICHMOND: Earl of Richmond

> Cibber's adaptation of Shakespeare's play extrapolates Richard's speech and adds a dialogue between Richard and Richmond that does not exist in the original. Here, after murdering and manipulating his way to becoming King, Richard and Richmond meet at Bosworth Field for a fight to the death to determine who will reign.

> Suggested weapons: broadsword, rapier

Bosworth Field. Enter Richard in disorder.

RICHARD: A Horse! a Horse! My Kingdom for a Horse!
Slave, I have set my Life upon a Cast,
And I will stand the hazard of the Dye.
I think there be six Richmonds in the Field;
Five have I slain to day, instead of him.
A Horse! a Horse! my Kingdom for a Horse.
(Enter Richmond.)
Of one, or both of us the time is come.
RICHMOND: Kind Heaven I thank thee, for my Cause is thine;
If Richard's fit to live let Richmond fall.
RICHARD: Thy Gallant bearing, Harry, I cou'd plaud,
But that the spotted Rebel stains the Soldier.
RICHMOND: Nor shou'd thy Prowess, Richard, want my praise,
But that thy cruel deeds have stampt thee Tyrant.
So thrive my Sword as Heaven's high Vengeance draws it.
RICHARD: "My Soul and Body on the Action both."
RICHMOND: A dreadful lay: Here's to decide it.

(Alarm, fight.)

RICHARD: Perdition catch thy Arm. The chance is thine:
(Richard is wounded.)
But oh! the vast Renown thou hast acquired
In Conquering Richard, does afflict him more
Than even his Bodies parting with its Soul:
"Now let the World no longer be a Stage
"To feed contention in a lingring Act:
"But let one spirit of the First-born Cain
"Reign in all bosoms, that each heart being set
"On bloody Actions, the rude Scene may end,
"And darkness be the Burier of the Dead."
(Dies.)

RICHMOND: Farewell, Richard, and from thy dreadful end
May future Kings from Tyranny be warn'd;
Had thy aspiring Soul but stir'd in Vertue
With half the Spirit it has dar'd in Evil,
How might thy Fame have grac'd our English Annals:
But as thou art, how fair a Page thou'st blotted.
Hark! the glad Trumpets speak the Field our own.

❖ ❖ ❖

Box and Cox
by John Maddison Morton, Esq. (1847)

JOHN BOX: a journeyman printer
JAMES COX: a journeyman hatter

> Box and Cox have found out that they have been duped by
> their landlady and are actually renting the same room —
> one by night and the other by day. They have also discov-
> ered that they have both been engaged to the same girl at
> different times. Box left her at the altar and Cox does not
> want her now. They argue to determine who will have to
> go back to her.

> Suggested weapons: found

> *An upstairs room in a rooming house.*

BOX: I say, sir!

COX: Well, sir?

BOX: What's your opinion of duelling, sir?

COX: I think it's a barbarous practice, sir.

BOX: So do I, sir. To be sure, I don't so much object to it when
the pistols are not loaded.

COX: No, I dare say that *does* make a difference.

BOX: And yet, sir — on the other hand — doesn't it strike you
a rather a waste of time, for two people to keep firing pistols at another, with nothing in 'em?

COX: No, sir — no more than any other harmless recreation.

BOX: Hark ye! Why do you object to marry Penelope Ann?

COX: Because, as I've observed already, I can't abide her. You'll
be happy with her.

BOX: Happy? Me! With the consciousness that I have deprived
you of such a treasure? No, no, Cox!

COX: Don't think of me, Box — I shall be sufficiently rewarded by the knowledge of my Box's happiness.

BOX: Don't be absurd, sir!

COX: Then don't you be ridiculous, sir!

BOX: I won't have her!

COX: I won't have her!

BOX: I have it! Suppose we draw lots for the lady — eh, Mr. Cox?

COX: That's fair enough Mr. Box.

BOX: Or, what say you to dice?

COX: With all my heart! Dice, by all means. *(Eagerly.)*

BOX: *(Aside.)* That's lucky! Mrs. Bouncer's nephew left a pair here yesterday. He sometimes persuades me to have a throw for a trifle, and as he always throws sixes, I suspect they are good ones.

(Goes to the cupboard at right, and brings out the dice-box.)

COX: *(Aside.)* I've no objection at all to dice. I lost one pound, seventeen and sixpence, at last Barnet Races, to a very gentlemanly looking man, who had a most peculiar knack of throwing sixes; I suspected they were loaded, so I gave him another half-crown, and he gave me the dice.

(Takes dice out of his pocket — uses lucifer box as substitute for dice-box, which is on table.)

BOX: Now then, sir!

COX: I'm ready, sir! *(They seat themselves at opposite sides of the table.)* Will you lead off, sir?

BOX: As you please, sir. The lowest throw, of course, wins Penelope Ann?

COX: Of course, sir.

BOX: Very well, sir!

COX: Very well, sir!

BOX: *(Rattling dice and throwing.)* Sixes!

COX: That's not a bad throw of yours, sir. *(Rattling dice — throws.)* Sixes!

BOX: That's a pretty good one of yours, sir. *(Throws.)* Sixes!

COX: *(Throws.)* Sixes!

BOX: Sixes!

COX: Sixes!

BOX: Sixes!

COX: Sixes!

BOX: Those are not bad dice of yours, sir.

COX: Yours seem pretty good ones, sir.

BOX: Suppose we change?

COX: Very well, sir. *(They change dice.)*

BOX: *(Throwing.)* Sixes!

COX: Sixes!

BOX: Sixes!

COX: Sixes!

BOX: *(Flings down the dice.)* Pooh! It's perfectly absurd, your going on throwing sixes in this sort of way, sir!

COX: I shall go on till my luck changes, sir!

BOX: Let's try something else. I have it! Suppose we toss for Penelope Ann?

COX: The very thing I was going to propose!
(They each turn aside and take out a handful of money.)

BOX: *(Aside, examining money.)* Where's my tossing shilling? Here it is.

COX: *(Aside, examining money.)* Where's my lucky sixpence? I've got it.

BOX: Now then, sir, heads wins?

COX: Or tails lose, whichever you prefer.

BOX: It's the same to me, sir.

COX: Very well, sir — heads I win; tails you lose.

BOX: Yes. *(Suddenly.)* No — heads wins, sir.

COX: Very well — go on.

BOX: *(Tossing.)* Heads!

COX: *(Tossing.)* Heads!

BOX: *(Tossing.)* Heads!

COX: *(Tossing.)* Heads!

BOX: Ain't you rather tired of turning up heads, sir?

COX: Couldn't you vary the monotony of our proceedings by an occasional tail, sir?

BOX: *(Tossing.)* Heads!

COX: *(Tossing.)* Heads!

BOX: Heads? Stop, sir! Will you permit me? *(Taking Cox's sixpence.)* Holloa! Your sixpence has got no tail, sir!

COX: *(Seizing Box's shilling.)* And your shilling has got two heads, sir!

BOX: Cheat!

COX: Swindler!

(They are about to rush upon each other, then retreat to some distance, and commence sparring, and striking fiercely at one another.)

❖ ❖ ❖

Cyrano de Bergerac
by Edmond Rostand (1897)
translated by Charles Marowitz

CYRANO DE BERGERAC
VICOMPTE DE VALVERT

> After Cyrano publicly orders the actor, Monfleury, to leave
> the stage at the Hotel de Bourgogne, the angry nobleman,
> Valvert, attempts to insult Cyrano by calling attention to
> his nose. Cyrano, the most famous swordsman of France,
> responds by suggesting a duel to end the dispute, during
> which he will recite a poem to be completed by a wound
> to Valvert. (Note: Some versions of this fight have the final
> thrust to Valvert be a kill.)

> Suggested weapons: rapiers

> *Paris, the Hall of the Hotel de Bourgogne.*

VALVERT: *(All choked up.)*
　　What arrogance; what airs!
　　A clown — just look at him — no gloves — no lace —
　　No buckles on his shoes — no handkerchief.
CYRANO:
　　My adornments are not visible.
　　I wear them all within. *(Hand to heart.)* Nor am I
　　Caparisoned like a circus horse —
　　Or stuffed with feathers like a popinjay.
　　But you'll look in vain to find an insult
　　That I have not with valor washed away.
　　You'll find no ling'ring bile within my conscience;
　　No honor frayed — no scruples cast aside.
　　I glisten with bright emeralds unseen,
　　My white plumes of freedom all embossed

With my good name. — No, not a stalkinghorse,
But a soul in shining armor, arrayed
With deeds, not decorations. Twirling my wit
Like moustachioes that go before me
A deadly pair of swinging scimitars.
A nerve of steel that throbs within my scabbard
And, upon the clattering cobblestones,
The echo of my bold, unvarnished truths
Reverberating like an Angelus.

VALVERT:

However . . .

CYRANO: (Deprecatingly.)

I haven't any gloves, alas.
I did have one — the last of one old pair,
But lost it rather carelessly I fear.
A varlet dropped an insult I found base,
And I'm afraid, I left it in his face.

VALVERT:

Dolt! Knave! Wastrel! Booby! Clod!

CYRANO: (Assuming Valvert has just introduced himself, Cyrano doffs his hat and does the same.)

And I, Cyrano-Savinien-Hercule De Bergerac.

VALVERT: (Incensed.)

Buffoon! Jackanape!

CYRANO: (Suddenly shrieks out loud as if with pain.)

Aghhh!

VALVERT:

Now what?

CYRANO: (Grimacing with false pain.)

These horrid cramps will be the death of me.
I've left it too long idle.

VALVERT:

What's he saying?

CYRANO: (Now grim.)

My sword has gone to sleep.

VALVERT: *(Drawing his own sword.)*
    I see. Well then,
    I'll rouse it soon enough.
CYRANO: *(Meticulously.)*
    I solemnly vow
    To transport you exquisitely into
    The Other World.
VALVERT:

                    Vain, poetic braggart!

CYRANO:
    Indeed a poet, and to demonstrate
    My skill will, as I flay you, improvise
    A ballade, extempore.
VALVERT:

                  A ballade?

CYRANO: *(Pedantically.)*
    Which, you may or may not know, consists
    Of three eight-lined stanzas and refrain
    Containing four . . .
VALVERT:

                Enough waffle, sir.

CYRANO:
    I'll create it as we duel and when the last
    Line comes around — thrust home.
VALVERT: *(Narky.)*

                    Will you?

CYRANO:

                    I will.

    (Declaiming.)
    "Ballade of the Duel at the Hotel Bourgogne
    Between de Bergerac and a Boetian."
VALVERT: What's that supposed to mean?
CYRANO: *(With withering scorn.)*
            The title, m'sieur.

(Tableau: A huddle of people forms in the center of the floor with the Marquis and Officers mingling with the citizens and others in the inn. Some of the Pages mount the shoulders of onlookers to get a better view; in the boxes, the ladies raise their lorgnettes and lean over expectantly. De Guiche and his entourage are on the right; Le Bret, Cuigy, Ragueneau, and others of Cyrano's persuasion, to the left.)

CYRANO: A moment while I choose my rhymes.
(Cyrano places two fingers to his brow and, with poetic concentration, slowly shuts his eyes. Having consulted his Muse, he then opens them wide.)
Allons!
(Throughout, he suits the action to the word.)
First I doff my old chapeau,
My ancient cape (that's slightly frayed),
And as I measure up my foe,
I send my voice into my blade.
A Lancelot reborn am I,
Hear my saber swish and whoosh!
Like Spartacus, I twirl and fly
More agile I, than Scaramouche.
(They cross swords; the duel starts in earnest.)
Where shall I skewer this popinjay
(This poor misguided upstart crow)
In his bosom, shall we say;
In his belly or below?
Can you hear my saber's call
As I intone this jolly poem.
Now you're backed against the wall,
And soon enough, I will thrust home.
Your complexion's getting very pale
Your breathing's short, and it's my hunch
It's something indigestible
You may perchance have had for lunch.

(Beats down Valvert's sword with a two-handed blow.)
Sorry for that sudden crunch
I didn't mean to hit your dome
We poets're such a rowdy bunch,
But soon enough, I will thrust home.
(Cyrano throws some fast passes at his adversary, which he parries with some difficulty, then stops abruptly and says with great solemnity:)
O God, I fear the time has come
To end this fateful little poem.
The end is sad and rather glum.
With one last flourish . . .
(He lunges; Valvert staggers back and falls into the arms of his friends. Cyrano recovers, salutes.)
I thrust home!

❖ ❖ ❖

Les Liaisons Dangereuses
by Christopher Hampton (1984)

LE VICOMPTE DE VALMONT
LE CHEVALIER DANCENY
AZOLAN: Valmont's man
MANSERVANT: Danceny's servant

After discovering that Valmont has been having an affair with his love Cecile, Danceny has challenged Valmont, a swordsman of much more experience, to a duel of honour.

Suggested weapons: epée, small sword

Down on a misty December morning in the Bois de Vincennes. On one side of the stage, Valmont and Azolan; on the other, Danceny and a Manservant. Valmont is making his selection from a case of epées, held open for him by Azolan. He weighs now one and now the other in his hand. Danceny, meanwhile, waits impatiently, in shirt-sleeves, epée in hand, shifting from one foot to the other. Finally, as Valmont seems to be on the point of making his decision, Danceny can restrain himself no further.

DANCENY: I know it was easy for you to make a fool of me when I trusted you, but out here I think you'll find there's very little room for trickery!
(His Manservant looks at him disapprovingly, but Valmont responds calmly to this breach of etiquette.)
VALMONT: I recommend you conserve your energy for the business at hand.
(He makes his final choice of epée and lays it on the ground while Azolan helps him off with his coat and on with a black glove. Then, Valmont and Danceny approach one another and take up the en-garde position. At a sign

from Azolan, the duel begins, fierce and determined, Valmont's skill against Danceny's aggression. For some time, they're evenly matched, with Valmont, if anything, looking the more dangerous. Then Danceny succeeds, more by luck than good judgment, in wounding Valmont in whichever is not his sword arm. A short pause ensues and then, after a murmured consultation between Valmont and Azolan, the duellists resume the en-garde position and begin again. This time it's Danceny who looks to have the initiative. For some reason, connected or not with his wound, Valmont seems to have lost heart, or even interest, and at one point when the deflection of a too-committed attack by Danceny seems to leave him wide open, Valmont fails to take advantage of what looks like a golden opportunity. Eventually, it's some piece of inattention very close to carelessness on Valmont's part that allows Danceny through his guard with a thrust that enters Valmont's body somewhere just below his heart. There's a moment of mutual shock, and then Danceny withdraws his sword and Valmont staggers a couple of steps towards him, before subsiding with a slight gasp to the ground. Azolan hurries to him, falls to one knee, and lifts Valmont's head.)

VALMONT: I'm cold.

(Azolan runs to get Valmont's coat, as Danceny turns to his Manservant.)

DANCENY: Fetch the surgeon!

VALMONT: No, no.

DANCENY: Do as I say.

(The Manservant hurries away as Azolan manages to drape Valmont's coat around him. Danceny stands alone, uneasy, some way off, so that Valmont has to make the considerable effort to raise his voice above a murmur to be sure that Danceny will hear him.)

VALMONT: A moment of your time.

(Danceny reluctantly approaches. Valmont begins to try to

struggle up on one elbow, and Azolan drops to one knee to support him.)

Two things: a word of advice, which of course you may ignore, but it is honestly intended; and a request. *(He pauses, a little breathless.)*

DANCENY: Go on.

VALMONT: The advice is: be careful of the Marquise de Merteuil.

DANCENY: You must permit me to treat with skepticism anything you have to say about her.

VALMONT: Nevertheless, I must tell you: In this affair, both of us are her creatures.

(Danceny looks at him thoughtfully, not answering for a moment.)

DANCENY: And the request?

VALMONT: I want you to get somehow to see Madame de Tourvel . . .

DANCENY: I understand she is very ill.

VALMONT: That's why this is most important to me. I want you to tell her I can't explain why I broke with her as I did, but that since then, my life has been worth nothing. I pushed the blade in deeper than you just did, my boy, and I want you to help me withdraw it. Tell her it's lucky for her that I've gone and I'm glad not to have to live without her. Tell her her love was the only real happiness I've ever known.

DANCENY: I will.

VALMONT: Thank you.

(The silence is broken by snatches of birdsong. Danceny, suddenly overcome, puts a hand up to brush away a tear. Azolan, watching, lets his indignation show.)

AZOLAN: It's all very well doing that now.

VALMONT: Let him be. He had good cause. It's something I don't believe anyone's ever been able to say about me.

(He raises a hand towards Danceny: but the effort of doing so is too great, and he slumps back before Danceny can take his hand. He's dead.)

❖ ❖ ❖

Scenes for Two Women

❖　❖　❖

The Taming of the Shrew
by William Shakespeare (c. 1593)
edited by Don Weingust

KATHERINE
BIANCA
BAPTISTA

Envious of her younger sister having suitors, the shrewish Katherine resorts to inflicting physical harm. Bianca tries to bargain her way out of bondage, but to no avail. Their father arrives and upbraids Katherine for torturing her sister. Katherine responds by alleging that their father has greater love for Bianca, and as a result, Katherine will be forced to "dance barefoot" at her younger sister's wedding (the proverbial custom for an unwed elder sister) and ultimately, rather than being led into heaven by children, suffer the old maid's indignity of leading "apes in [to] hell."

Suggested weapon: rope

Padua. A room in Baptista's house. Enter Katherine and Bianca.

BIANCA: Good sister, wrong me not, nor wrong yourself,
　　To make a bondmaid and a slave of me
　　That I disdain; but for these other goods
　　Unbind my hands, I'll pull them off myself,
　　Yea all my raiment, to my petticoat,
　　Or what you will command me will I do,
　　So well I know my duty to my elders.
KATE: Of all thy suitors here I charge tell
　　Whom thou lov'st best: see thou dissemble not.
BIANCA: Believe me sister, of all the men alive,
　　I never yet beheld that special face,

Which I could fancy more than any other.

KATE: Minion thou liest: Is't not Hortensio?

BIANCA: If you affect him sister, here I swear
I'll plead for you my self but you shall have him.

KATE: O then belike you fancy riches more,
You will have Gremio to keep you fair.

BIANCA: Is it for him you do envy me so?
Nay, then you jest, and now I well perceive
You have but jested with me all this while:
I prithee sister Kate, untie my hands.

KATE: If that be jest, then all the rest was so.
(Strikes her.)
(Enter Baptista.)

BAPTISTA: Why how now Dame, whence grows this insolence?
Bianca stand aside, poor girl she weeps:
Go ply thy Needle, meddle not with her.
For shame thou Hilding of a devilish spirit,
Why dost thou wrong her, that did ne'er wrong thee?
When did she cross thee with a bitter word?

KATE: Her silence flouts me, and I'll be reveng'd.
(Flies after Bianca.)

BAPTISTA: What in my sight? Bianca get thee in.
(Bianca exits.)

KATE: What will you not suffer me: Nay now I see
She is your treasure, she must have a husband,
I must dance barefoot on her wedding day,
And for your love to her, lead Apes in hell.
Talk not to me, I will go sit and weep,
Till I can find occasion of revenge.

BAPTISTA: Was ever Gentleman thus griev'd as I?

❖ ❖ ❖

Ring Around the Moon
by Jean Anouilh
adapted by Christopher Fry (1950)

DIANA MESSERSCHMANN: engaged to Frederic, daughter
of the richest man in the world
ISABELLE: a ballet dancer
JOSHUA

As a challenge, Frederic's twin brother, Horace, has ar-
ranged for a beautiful ballet dancer, Isabelle, to serve as a
foil at Frederic's engagement party to Diana, eager that Isabelle's beauty will deflect Frederick's attention from
Diana. After the scheme is successful, Diana bitterly con-
fronts Isabelle and tries to humiliate her regarding her
place in society.

Unarmed

*At the Château de Saint Fleur. Isabelle leans against down-
stage jalousie. Diana enters, stands for a moment looking
at Isabelle, who raises her head after a moment and sees
Diana.*

DIANA: It's quite true; you're wearing a most attractive dress.
ISABELLE: *(Moving left center.)* Yes, it is.
DIANA: *(Moving to right of Isabelle.)* And you're looking beautiful; that's true, too.
ISABELLE: Thank you. *(Diana moves above Isabelle, inspecting
her, then goes up steps. Isabelle eases center.)*
DIANA: Perhaps not perfectly groomed, still a little too close to
nature; and certainly not a very good powder, nor a very
good perfume.
ISABELLE: That must be why I find yours a little too good, and
you a little too far —

DIANA: Well? Too far what?

ISABELLE: — from nature.

DIANA: (Crossing below Isabelle.) You've managed quite well; (Moves below table down right.) but if one hasn't a maid who understands these things it's almost fatal; with the best will in the world one neglects oneself. No woman can tend herself and altogether survive. Do you get up early in the morning?

ISABELLE: (Moving to left. of Diana.) Yes.

DIANA: Yes, one can see.

ISABELLE: Do you go late to bed?

DIANA: Yes.

ISABELLE: Yes, one can see.

DIANA: (After slight pause.) Tell me, do you mind very much?

ISABELLE: Mind what?

DIANA: Wearing something you haven't made yourself?

ISABELLE: As a compensation, my eyelashes are my own.

DIANA: Happily for you. You'll need them tomorrow, without the help you get from the dress.

ISABELLE: I take it away with me. It was given me.

DIANA: That's very nice, isn't it? You'll be able to be a beauty all over again. I hear they're holding a jolly dance on the fourteenth day of July at St. Fleur. You'll turn all the bumpkins' heads. (Crosses below Isabelle to center.) Do you like my dress?

ISABELLE: Yes, it's most beautiful.

DIANA: Would you like it? I shall never wear it again. I hardly ever wear a dress more than once. Besides, I can't really tell myself I like petunia. Tomorrow I shall dine in rose-pink, rather a miracle dress, a harness of little pleats, twenty yards of them. If you come up to my room I'll show it to you. (Takes Isabelle by hand, draws her left center.) Yes, do come and see it; I'm sure it'll give you pleasure.

ISABELLE: (Withdrawing her hand.) No. (Backs to left of table down right.)

DIANA: Why not? Do you envy me? That's one of the sins, you

know. You'd love to be rich, wouldn't you? If this evening were only a true story, and you had as many dresses as I have.

ISABELLE: Naturally.

DIANA: But you'll never have more that one, isn't that so? *(Isabelle turns, moves above table down right toward exit right center. She moves quickly to left of Isabelle.)* And if I put my foot on your train *(Puts her foot on hem of Isabelle's frock.)* in this way — *(Isabelle stoops and turns.)* — and tug it a little, you'll not even have one.

ISABELLE: Take your foot away.

DIANA: No.

ISABELLE: Take your foot away or else I shall hit you.

DIANA: Don't squirm, you little fury; you'll do some damage. *(Isabelle pulls at frock and it tears.)*

ISABELLE: *(With a cry.)* Oh my dress!

DIANA: You did it yourself. *(Moves left of table up center.)* A few tacks, it will still do very nicely for St. Fleur. It's exciting, I expect, to have such a triumphant evening with a borrowed dress on your back. The pity is, it's over so soon. Tomorrow morning you have to pack your cardboard box, and I shall still be here, and that's the difference between us. *(Pours a glass of champagne for herself, goes up steps, leans against post right of them. A short pause. Isabelle looks at Diana, but without dislike.)*

ISABELLE: *(Suddenly.)* Is it so pleasant to be unpleasant? *(Moves below table up center.)*

DIANA: *(With a change of tone, sighing.)* No. But one can't always be pleased.

ISABELLE: Can you be unhappy as well? That's very strange. Why?

DIANA: I have too much money.

ISABELLE: But Frederic loves you.

DIANA: I don't love him. I love Hugo, and he dislikes my money, and I think he's right.

ISABELLE: Become poor then.

DIANA: Do you think it is so easy?

ISABELLE: *(Easing down center.)* I make no effort.

DIANA: *(Crossing to table down right.)* You don't know how lucky you are. *(Puts her glass on table.)* I suppose this is a lovely party — but all my friends give parties like it. *(Moves to right of table down right.)* I shall never again know the excitement of being invited up to the great house — and that's so sad.

ISABELLE: So sad.

DIANA: I tell you money is only worth something to the poor.

ISABELLE: Which proves there is something the matter with the world. I have been humiliated and hurt this evening, and my only dress has been torn, because I am one of the poor ones. *(Moves above chair left of table down right.)* I'm going to do what the poor ones always do. I'm leaving words for deeds, and asking you to go away.

DIANA: *(Sitting right of table down right.)* Go away? Do you think you're in your own home, you little adventuress?

ISABELLE: Go and cry over your millions somewhere a long way off. I'm pretty stupid and very ashamed to have spent so many minutes trying to understand you. So now I shall use the arguments of the poor. *(Moves below table down right.)* If you don't go I shall throw you out.

DIANA: Throw me out? I should like to see you try.

ISABELLE: You're going to see me try. And as you wouldn't care if I tore your dress, I shall tear your face instead: God has been unusually impartial, giving us one face each. *(Grabs Diana by the hair.)*

DIANA: *(Rising.)* You're a common little slut. Do you think I'm afraid? *(Kicks her chair away and with Isabelle still hanging on to her hair backs above table down right to right center drawing Isabelle with her.)*

ISABELLE: Not yet. But I think you may be.

DIANA: Oh! You'll ruin my hair.

ISABELLE: *(Pulling Diana's hair down.)* You have a maid to put it right. What does it matter? *(Releases Diana, backs down right.)*

DIANA: I've got claws as well as you.

ISABELLE: *(Rushing at Diana.)* Then use them. *(Diana seizes Isabelle's wrists, swings her round to center.)*

DIANA: I was poor once, myself. *(Stamps on Isabelle's right foot with her left. Isabelle yelps and breaks down left center.)* When I was ten, I fought all the little toughs on the docks at Istanbul. *(Isabelle runs at Diana. There is a sharp tussle in which they box each other's ears, and Diana pulls Isabelle's hair down. As they wrestle together, Joshua enters right center. As he sees them, he gives a yell of horror, crosses quickly, exits down left.)*

JOSHUA: *(As he exits, calling.)* Mr. Hugo! Mr. Hugo!

(Diana throws Isabelle to the ground, picks up the remains of some fruit from the table up center, throws it over Isabelle, then collapses left of her on the ground. Frederic enters down left, stands speechless with his back to the audience. Diana rises, moves below table down right to right of it.)

❖ ❖ ❖

A Taste of Honey
by Shelagh Delaney (1959)

HELEN: a semiwhore, under forty years old
JOSEPHINE: her daughter, eighteen years old

Jo has become engaged to a black sailor, who has just left for sea and will not return for six months. Hoping to assure that he will come back for her, she loses her virginity to him the night before. Helen, her saloon-frequenting mother, is engaged to a man much younger than she is and takes no responsibility for Jo at all. Today is Helen's wedding day, and her enthusiasm for this marriage is despised by Jo.

Unarmed

A comfortless flat in Manchester. Helen dances on with an assortment of fancy boxes, containing her wedding clothes.

HELEN: JO! JO! Come on. Be sharp now.
(Jo comes on in her pyjamas. She has a very heavy cold.)
For God's sake give me a hand. I'll never be ready. What time is it? Have a look at the church clock.
JO: A quarter past eleven, and the sun's coming out.
HELEN: Oh! Well, happy the bride the sun shines on.
JO: Yeah, and happy the corpse the rain rains on. You're not getting married in a church, are you?
HELEN: Why, are you coming to throw bricks at us? Of course not. Do I look all right? Pass me my fur. Oh! My fur! Do you like it?
JO: I bet somebody's missing their cat.
HELEN: It's a wedding present from that young man of mine. He spends his money like water, you know, penny-wise,

pound-foolish. Oh! I am excited. I feel twenty-one all over again. Oh! You would have to catch a cold on my wedding day. I was going to ask you to be my bridesmaid too.

JO: Don't talk daft.

HELEN: Where did you put my shoes? Did you clean 'em ? Oh! They're on my feet. Don't stand there sniffing, Jo. Use a handkerchief.

JO: I haven't got one.

HELEN: Use this, then. What's the matter with you? What are you trying to hide

JO: Nothing.

HELEN: Don't try to kid me. What is it? Come on, let's see.

JO: It's nothing. Let go of me. You're hurting.

HELEN: What's this?

JO: A ring.

HELEN: I can see it's a ring. Who give it to you?

JO: A friend of mine.

HELEN: Who? Come on. Tell me.

JO: You're hurting me.

(Helen breaks the cord and gets the ring.)

HELEN: You should have sewn some buttons on your pyjamas if you didn't want me to see. Who give it you?

JO: My boyfriend. He asked me to marry him.

HELEN: Well, you silly little bitch. You mean that lad you've been knocking about with while we've been away?

JO: Yes.

HELEN: I could choke you.

JO: You've already had a damn good try.

HELEN: You haven't known him five minutes. Has he really asked you to marry him?

JO: Yes.

HELEN: Well, thank God for the divorce courts! I suppose just because I'm getting married you think you should.

JO: Have you got the monopoly?

HELEN: You stupid little devil! What sort of a wife do you think you'd make? You're useless. It takes you all your time to look after yourself. I suppose you think you're in love. Anybody can fall in love, do you know that? But what do you know about the rest of it?

JO: Ask yourself.

HELEN: You know where that ring should be? In the ashcan with everything else. Oh! I could kill her, I could really.

JO: You don't half knock me about. I hope you suffer for it.

HELEN: I've done my share of suffering if I never do any more. Oh Jo, you're only a kid. Why don't you learn from my mistakes? It takes half your life to learn from your own.

JO: You leave me alone. Can I have my ring back, please?

HELEN: What a thing to happen just when I'm going to enjoy myself for a change.

JO: Nobody's stopping you.

HELEN: Yes, and as soon as my back's turned you'll be off with this sailor boy and ruin yourself for good.

JO: I'm already ruined.

HELEN: Yes, it's just the sort of thing you'd do. You make me sick.

JO: You've no need to worry, Helen. He's gone away. He may be back in six months, but there again, he may . . .

HELEN: Look, you're only young. Enjoy your life. Don't get trapped. Marriage can be hell for a kid.

JO: Can I have your hanky back?

HELEN: Where did you put it?

JO: This is your fault too.

HELEN: Everything's my fault. Show me your tongue.

JO: Breathing your flu bugs all over me.

HELEN: Yes, and your neck's red where I pulled that string.

JO: Will you get me a drink of water, Helen?

❖ ❖ ❖

Zastrozzi
by George F. Walker (1977)

JULIA: an aristocrat, a fair-haired beauty
MATILDA: a gypsy, a raven-haired beauty

> Victor has knocked out his master Verezzi, "the vision-
> ary," and dragged him to a dungeon with the hope of stop-
> ping him from fighting Zastrozzi, the vengeful master
> criminal of Europe who has been looking for Verezzi for
> years. Meanwhile, Zastrozzi's henchman, Bernardo, has
> kidnaped Julia and taken her to the same dungeon. Hav-
> ing just hit her, he leaves her there unconscious. In this
> scene, Julia wakes up and meets Matilda, Zastrozzi's long-
> time mistress who is jealous of Zastrozzi's interest inJulia's
> beauty and innocence. They both find Verezzi there.

Suggested weapon: knife

Italy, the 1890s. A dungeon. Julia groans, She slowly re-
gains consciousness and gets up. She makes her way
around the dungeon, sees Verezzi, and goes to him. She
kneels down and takes his pulse.

JULIA: What is happening to me? I go for a series of walks in
the street. Smile at two young men. One of them tells me
he is a visionary. The other abducts me and tells me he is
going to rape and murder me, not necessarily in that order.
Then he hits me like he would a man and knocks me un-
conscious. I wake up and find the young man who thinks
he is a visionary lying on the ground bleeding to death
from a head wound. What's happening to me?
(Matilda enters.)
MATILDA: You must be the virgin. The one with the marvelous
gentle sensuality.

JULIA: Who are you?

MATILDA: My name is Matilda. I am your competition. I have a sensuality which is not the least bit gentle.

JULIA: Really? What do you want?

MATILDA: I want to kill all the virgins in the world.

JULIA: Oh no. What's happening to me?

MATILDA: Unfortunately for you, we are both in love with the same man.

JULIA: *(Pointing to Verezzi.)* Him? I don't love him. I don't even like him.

MATILDA: Not him. Zastrozzi.

JULIA: I've heard of him. He's the one who is whispered about in polite society.

MATILDA: He is the evil genius of all Europe. A criminal. And I am a criminal too. We belong together. So we must fight and I must kill you.

JULIA: Why can't I just leave?

MATILDA: That won't do. Besides, I will enjoy killing you. It is women like you who make me look like a tart.

JULIA: Nonsense. It's the way you dress.

MATILDA: Stand up, you mindless virgin.

JULIA: *(Standing.)* Madame, I am neither mindless nor a virgin. I am merely a victim of bizarre circumstances. A product of healthy civilization thrown into a jungle of the deranged.

MATILDA: Yes, get angry. You are better when you are angry. If I were a man I would seduce you on the spot.

JULIA: That's perverse!

MATILDA: *(Taking a knife from under her skirts.)* Yes, get indignant. You are quite provocative when you are upset. Take off your clothes.

JULIA: Why?

MATILDA: We are going to make love.

JULIA: Oh no, we are not.

MATILDA: Yes, get confused. You are quite ridiculous when you are confused. And it is exactly the way someone like you should die. *(She advances.)*

JULIA: What are you doing?

MATILDA: We are going to fight. And we are going to stop fighting when one of us is dead.

JULIA: I would rather not. I would rather discuss some other possibility. I'm only seventeen years old. People tell me I have so much to live for.

MATILDA: Oh? Name something worth living for and I might spare your life.

JULIA: But how could I? A woman like you could never appreciate what I think is worth living for. No offense. But take your dress for example. I would live to dress much better than that.

MATILDA: You mindless, coy, disgusting virgin!

(Matilda attacks and they struggle. The knife falls and Julia scrambles after it. Matilda leaps on her and somehow Matilda is stabbed. She falls over dead. Julia feels her pulse.)

JULIA: Dead. Oh my God. *(She stands.)* What is happening to me? First a victim. Now a murderer! And I didn't even know her. This is grossly unfair. I'm young. I've had the proper education. My future was a pleasant rosy colour. I could see it in my head. It was a rosy colour. Very pretty. This is truly grossly unfair.

❖ ❖ ❖

Scenes for One Man
and One Woman

❖ ❖ ❖

The Deluge — Noah and His Sons

anonymous, Wakefield Pageant (c. 1400s)

NOAH
NOAH'S WIFE

> From the Towneley cycle, this version of Noah has been slightly modernized for easier playing. After speaking with God about what he must do to prepare for the flood, Noah meets with his wife to explain what must be done. His apprehension is justified as the true nature of their relationship is revealed.

> Suggested weapons: found; a belt, staff, or thong

NOAH: Lord, homeward will I haste as fast as I may. My wife
will I see and hear what she say.
And I am afraid there will be some fray
Between us both;
For she is full testy,
For little oft angry;
If anything wrong be
Soon is she wroth.
(Noah's wife enters.)
God speed, dear wife, how fare ye?
WIFE: Now, as ever might I thrive, the worst is when I see thee!
Do tell me quickly, where hast thou thus long been?
To death may we drive, or life, for thee, for want indeed.
When we sweat or toil,
Thou dost what thou think,
Yet of meat and of drink
Have we much need.
NOAH: Wife, we are hard put with tidings new.

WIFE: But thou were worthy to be clad in Stafford blue!
   For thou art always afraid, be it false or true.
   But, God knows, I am led, and that may I rue full ill;
   For I dare be thy pledge,
   From evening unto morrow
   Thou speakest ever of sorrow;
   God send thee for once thy fill!
   (To the audience.)
   We women may beware all ill husbands.
   I have one, by Mary, that loosed me of my bands!
   If he be vexed, I must tarry, howsoever it stands,
   With semblance full sorry, wringing both my hands
   For dread.
   But some other while,
   What with game and with guile,
   I shall smite and smile,
   And pay him as he deserves
NOAH: Hold thy tongue, ram skit, or I shall make thee still!
WIFE: By my thrift, if thou smite, I shall return the ill.
NOAH: We shall try it at once. Have at thee, Jill!
   (He strikes her.)
   Upon the bone shall it bite.
WIFE: Ah, so, marry! Thou smitest ill,
   But I suppose
   I shall not in thy debt
   Get off this floor!
   Take thee here this thong
   To tie up thy hose.
   (She strikes back with a strap or thong.)
NOAH: Ah, wilt thou so? Marry, that is mine. *(Hits her.)*
WIFE: Thou shalt have three for two I swear by God's pain!
   (Hits back.)
NOAH: And I shall repay you those, in faith, ere long. *(Strikes her down.)*
WIFE: Out upon thee, ho!
NOAH: Thou canst both bite and whine

With a howl.
(To the audience.)
For if she wants to strike,
Yet fast will she screech.
In faith, I hold none of her like
In all the world!
But I will keep charity, for I have work to do.

WIFE: Here shall no man stop thee; I pray thee go to!
Full well if we miss thee, as ever have I peace.
To spin will I now do.

NOAH: Wey! Farewell, lo.
But wife,
Pray for me busily
Until I come again unto thee.

WIFE: For all thou wouldst prayest for me,
Well might I thrive.
(She exits.)

❖ ❖ ❖

Henry VI, Part 1
by William Shakespeare (c. 1590)
edited by Don Weingust

JOAN DE PUZEL
CHARLES LE DAUPHIN

Near the beginning of this rollicking history, the playwright brings together Charles, the heir to the French throne (the Dauphin, or "Dolphin"), and the young woman who believes herself to be ordained by God as France's deliverer from the English, Joan de Pucelle (or "Puzel"), now more familiarly known as Saint Joan of Arc. Charles agrees to fight with Joan as a test of her claims and is vanquished. In defeat his intentions turn amorous, but Joan politely sets aside this advance, pledging her honor to his military efforts.

Suggested weapons: broadswords, shield

JOAN: Dolphin, I am by birth a Shepherd's Daughter,
    My wit untrain'd in any kind of Art:
    Heaven and our Lady gracious hath it pleas'd
    To shine on my contemptible estate.
    Lo, whilest I waited on my tender Lambs,
    And to Sun's parching heat display'd my cheeks,
    God's Mother deigned to appear to me,
    And in a Vision full of Majesty,
    Will'd me to leave my base Vocation,
    And free my Country from Calamity:
    Her aid she promis'd, and assur'd success.
    In complete Glory she reveal'd herself:
    And whereas I was black and swart before,
    With those clear Rays, which she infus'd on me,
    That beauty am I blest with, which you may see.

Ask me what question thou canst possible,
And I will answer unpremeditated:
My Courage try by Combat, if thou dar'st,
And thou shalt find that I exceed my Sex.
Resolve on this, thou shalt be fortunate,
If thou receive me for thy Warlike Mate.

CHARLES: Thou hast astonisht me with thy high terms:
Only this proof I'll of thy Valour make,
In single Combat thou shalt buckle with me;
And if thou vanquishest, thy words are true,
Otherwise I renounce all confidence.

JOAN: I am prepar'd: here is my keen-edg'd Sword,
Deckt with fine Flower-de-Luces on each side,
The which at Touraine, in St. Katherines Church-yard,
Out of a great deal of old Iron, I chose forth.

CHARLES: Then come a God's name, I fear no woman.

JOAN: And while I live, I'll ne'er fly from a man.
(Here they fight, and Joan de Puzel overcomes.)

CHARLES: Stay, stay thy hands, thou art an Amazon,
And fightest with the Sword of Deborah.

JOAN: Christ's Mother helps me, else I were too weak.

CHARLES: Who e'er helps thee, 'tis thou that must help me:
Impatiently I burn with thy desire,
My heart and hands thou hast at once subdu'd.
Excellent Puzel, if thy name be so,
Let me thy servant, and not Sovereign be,
'Tis the French Dolphin sueth to thee thus.

JOAN: I must not yield to any rights of Love,
For my Profession's sacred from above:
When I have chased all thy Foes from hence,
Then will I think upon a recompence.

CHARLES: Mean time look gracious on thy prostrate Thrall.

❖ ❖ ❖

Soliman and Perseda
by Thomas Kyd (c. 1592)

SOLIMAN: Emperor of the Turks
PERSEDA: beloved of Erastus

Soliman lays siege on Rhodes and allows Erastus, whom he grows to like, to remain as one of his knights. Perseda, in love with Erastus, becomes one of Soliman's prisoners. He falls in love with her, but recognizing that Perseda will never marry him while Erastus is alive, Soliman reunites them but plots to accuse Erastus of treason to dishonor his name. He then strangles Erastus and kills all the men that helped him do it to secure the secret. Here, Perseda has figured out what has transpired.

Suggested weapon: broadsword

Outside Rhodes. The drum sounds a parley. Perseda comes upon the walls in man's apparel.

PERSEDA: At whose entreaty is this parley sounded?
SOLIMAN: At our entreaty; therefore yield the town.
PERSEDA: Why, what art thou that boldly bid us yield?
SOLIMAN: Great Soliman, Lord of all the world.
PERSEDA: Thou art not Lord of all; Rhodes is not thine.
SOLIMAN: It was, and shall be, maugre who says no.
PERSEDA: I, that say no, will never see it thine.
SOLIMAN: Why, what art thou that dares resist my force?
PERSEDA: A Gentleman, and thy mortal enemy.
    And one that dares thee to a single combat.
SOLIMAN: First tell me, doth Perseda live or no?
PERSEDA: She lives to see wrack of Soliman.
SOLIMAN: Then I will combat thee, what ere thou art.
PERSEDA: And in Erastus name I'll combat thee;
    And here I promise thee on my Christian faith,
    Then I will yield Perseda to thy hands,
    If that thy strength shall over match my right,

To use as to thy liking shall seem best.
But ere I come to enter single fight,
First let my tongue utter my heart's despight;
And thus my tale begins: thou wicked tyrant,
Thou murderer, accursed homicide,
For whom hell gapes, and all the ugly fiends
Do wait for to receive thee in their jaws:
Ah, purjured and inhuman Soliman,
How could thy heart harbour a wicked thought
Against the spotless life of poor Erastus?
In slaughtering him thy virtues are defamed:
Didst thou misdo him in hope to win Perseda?
Ah, foolish man, therein thou are deceived;
For, though she live, yet will she near live thine;
Which to approve, I'll come to combat thee,

SOLIMAN: Injurious, foul-mouthed knight, my wrathful arm
Shall chastise and rebuke these injuries.
(Then Perseda comes down to Soliman.)
I'll not defend Erastus innocence,
But die maintaining of Perseda's beauty.
(Then they fight; Soliman kills Perseda.)

PERSEDA: I, now I lay Perseda at thy feet,
But with thy hand first wounded to the death:
Now shall the world report that Soliman
Slew Erastus in hope to win Perseda,
And murdered her for loving of her husband.

SOLIMAN: What, my Perseda? Ah, what have I done?
Yet kiss me, gentle love, before thou die.

PERSEDA: A kiss I grant thee, though I hate thee deadly.

SOLIMAN: I loved thee dearly, and accept thy kiss.
Why didst thou love Erastus more than me?
Or why didst not give Soliman a kiss
Ere this unhappy time? Then hadst thou lived.
Ah, Perseda, how shall I mourn for thee?
(She dies.)

❖ ❖ ❖

Alphonsus, King of Aragon
by Robert Greene (1599)

ALPHONSUS: son of Carinus, the rightful heir to the crown
of Aragon
IPHIGENA: daughter to Amurack, the Great Turk

After taking back the Kingdom of Aragon, previously
taken from his family, Alphonsus gains power over Milan
and Naples as well. Determined to also gain control of
Turkey, Alphonsus captures Amurack, the Turkish King,
and sets his sights on Iphigena, Amurack's daughter. She
will not give in easily, and here we find her fighting
Alphonsus to keep her freedom.

Suggested weapons: rapiers, dagger

Alarum: Alphonsus flies, followed by Iphigena.

IPHIGENA: How now, Alphonsus! You which never yet
Could meet your equal in the feats of arms,
How haps it now that in such sudden sort
You fly the presence of a silly maid?
What, have you found mine arm of such a force
As that you think your body over-weak
For to withstand the fury of my blows?
Or do you else disdain to fight with me,
For staining of your high nobility?
ALPHONSUS: No, dainty dame, I would not have thee think
That ever though or any other wight
Shall live to see Alphonsus fly the field
From any king or keisar whosome'er:
First I will die in the thickest of my foe.
Before I will debase mine honour so.

Nor do I scorn, thou goddess, for to stain
My prowess with thee, although it be a shame
For knights to combat with the female sect:
But love, sweet mouse, hath so benumb'd my wit,
That, though I would, I must refrain from it.

IPHIGENA: I thought as much when first I came to wars;
Your noble acts were fitter to be writ
Within the tables of Dame Venus' son
Than in God Mars his warlike registers:
Whenas your lords are hacking helms abroad,
And make their spears to shiver in the air,
Your mind is busied in fond Cupid's toys.
Come on i'faith, I'll teach you for to know,
We came to fight, and not to love, I trow.

ALPHONSUS: Nay, virgin, stay. An if thou wilt vouchsafe
To entertain Alphonsus' simple suit,
Thou shalt ere long be monarch of the world:
All christened kings, with all your pagan dogs,
Shall bend their knees unto Iphigena;
The Indian soil shall be thine at command,
Where every step thou settest on the ground
Shall be receivèd on the golden mines;
Rich Pactolus, that river of account,
Which doth descend from top of Tmolus Mount,
Shall be thine own, and all the world beside,
If you will grant to be Alphonsus' bride.

IPHIGENA: Alphonsus' bride! Nay villain, do not think
That fame or riches can so rule my thoughts
As for to make me love and fancy him
Whom I do hate, and in such sort despise,
As if my death could bring to pass his bane,
I would not long from Pluto's port remain.

ALPHONSUS: Nay, then, proud peacock, since thou art so stout
As that entreaty will not move thy mind
For to consent to be my wedded spouse,

Thou shalt, in spite of gods and fortune too,
Serve high Alphonsus as a concubine.

IPHIGENA: I'd rather die that ever that shall hap.

ALPHONSUS: And thou shalt die unless it come to pass.

(Alphonsus and Iphigena fight. Iphigena flies, followed by Alphonsus.)

❖ ❖ ❖

The Roaring Girl
by Thomas Middleton and Thomas Dekker (1611)

MOLL CUTPURSE: the Roaring Girl
LAXTON: a lewd

> Laxton, captivated by Moll, a pipe-smoking, cross-dressing cutpurse, approaches her to serve as his whore in the back of a coach. She agrees, but arrives in man's attire, ready to fight him as a spokesperson for all women who have been treated as such.

> Suggested weapons: short sword, rapier

London, Gray's Inn Fields.

LAXTON: Stay, 'tis now about the hour of her appointment, but yet I see her not. *(The clock strikes three.)* Hark what's this? One, two, three, three by the clock at Savoy; this is the hour, and Gray's Inn Fields the place, she swore she'd meet me: ha, yonder's two Inns o' Court men with one wench, but that's not she, they walk toward Islington out of my way: I see none yet dressed like her, I must look for a shag ruff, a frieze jerkin, a short sword, and a saveguard, or I get none: why Moll, prithee make haste, or the coachman will curse us anon.
(Enter Moll like a man.)

MOLL: *(Aside.)* Oh, here's my gentleman: if they would keep their days as well with their mercers as their hours with their harlots, no bankrupt would give seven score pound for a sergeant's place, for would you know a catchpoll rightly deriv'd, the corruption of a citizen is the generation of a sergeant! How his eye hawks for venery! — Come, are you ready, sir?

LAXTON: Ready? For what, sir?

MOLL: Do you ask that now, sir? Why was this meeting 'pointed?

LAXTON: I thought you mistook me, sir.
You seem to be some young barrister.
I have no suit in law; all my land's sold:
I praise heaven for't; 't has rid me of much trouble.

MOLL: Then I must wake you, sir. Where stands the coach?

LAXTON: Who's this? Moll? Honest Moll?

MOLL: So young and purblind? You're an old wanton in your eyes, I see that.

LAXTON: Th' art admirably suited for the Three Pigeons at Brainford; I'll swear I knew thee not.

MOLL: I'll swear you did not, but you shall know me now.

LAXTON: No, not here, we shall be spied, i'faith; the coach is better, come.

MOLL: Stay.

LAXTON: What, wilt thou untruss a point, Moll?
(She puts off her cloak and draws.)

MOLL: Yes, here's the point that I untruss, it has but one tag; 'twill serve tho' to tie up a rogue's tongue.

LAXTON: How!

MOLL: There's the gold with which you hir'd your hackney.
(Attacking him.) Here's her pace;
She racks hard, and perhaps your bones will feel it!
Ten angels of mine own I've put to thine;
Win 'em and wear 'em!

LAXTON: Hold, Moll, Mistress Mary!

MOLL: Draw or I'll serve an execution on thee
Shall lay thee up till doomsday!

LAXTON: Draw upon a woman? Why, what dost mean, Moll?

MOLL: To teach thy base thoughts manners. Th' art one of those
That thinks each woman thy fond, flexible whore,
If she but cast a liberal eye upon thee;
Turn back her head, she's thine: or, amongst company,
By chance drink first to thee, then she's quite gone,

There's no means to help her; nay for a need,
Wilt swear unto thy credulous fellow lechers
That art more in favour with a lady
At first sight than her monkey all her lifetime.
There's no mercy in't. — What durst move you, sir,
To think me whorish?
I scorn to prostitute myself to a man,
I, that can prostitute a man to me:
And so I greet thee.

LAXTON: Hear me.

MOLL: Would the spirits
Of all my slanderers were clasp'd in thine,
That I might vex an army at one time.

LAXTON: I do repent me! Hold!
(They fight.)

MOLL: You'll die the better Christian then.

LAXTON: I do confess I have wrong'd thee, Moll.

MOLL: Confession is but poor amends for wrong,
Unless a rope would follow.

LAXTON: I ask thee pardon.

MOLL: I'm your hir'd whore, sir.

LAXTON: I yield both purse and body!

MOLL: Both are mine and now at my disposing.

LAXTON: Spare my life!

MOLL: I scorn to strike thee basely.

LAXTON: Spoke like a noble girl, i' faith! *(Aside.)* Heart, I think
I fight with a familiar or the ghost of a fencer! Sh' has
wounded me gallantly. Call you this a lecherous voyage?
Here's blood would have serv'd me this seven year in bro-
ken heads and cut fingers, and it now runs all out together.
Pox o' the Three Pigeons! I would the coach were here
now to carry me to the surgeon's.
(Exit Laxton.)

MOLL: If I could meet my enemies one by one thus,
I might make pretty shift with 'em in time,
And make 'em know, she that has wit and spirit

May scorn to live beholding to her body for meat,
Or for apparel like your common dame
That makes shame get her clothes to cover shame.
Base is that mind that kneels unto her body,
As if a husband stood in awe on's wife:
My spirit shall be mistress of this house
As long as I have time in't.

❖ ❖ ❖

The Beaux Stratagem
by George Farquar (1707)

MRS. SULLEN: married to Mr. Sullen, a country blockhead
ARCHER: a gentleman of broken fortune

> After squandering all their money in London, Aimwell and
> Archer have descended on the provincial town of Lichfield.
> Posing as master and servant, their plan is for one of them
> to secure a lucrative marriage and split the income. Here,
> Archer has attempted an illicit "courtship" with the un-
> happily married Mrs. Sullen.

> Suggested weapons: found

> *A bedchamber in Lady Bountiful's house. Enter Mrs.
> Sullen, undressed.*

MRS. SULLEN: Thoughts free! Are they so? Why, then, suppose
him here, dressed like a youthful, gay, and burning bride-
groom, *(Here Archer steals out of the closet.)* with tongue
enchanting, eyes bewitching, knees imploring — *(Turns a
little o' one side, and sees Archer in the posture she de-
scribes.)* — Ah! — *(Shrieks and runs to the other side of
the stage.)* Have my thoughts raised a spirit? — What are
you, sir, a man or a devil?

ARCHER: A man, a man, madam. *(Rising.)*

MRS. SULLEN: How shall I be sure of it?

ARCHER: Madam, I'll give you demonstration this minute.
(Takes her hand.)

MRS. SULLEN: What, sir! Do you intend to be rude?

ARCHER: Yes, madam, if you please.

MRS. SULLEN: In the name of wonder, whence came ye?

ARCHER: From the skies, madam — I'm a Jupiter in love, and
you shall be my Alemena.

MRS. SULLEN: How came you in?

ARCHER: I flew in at the window, madam; your cousin Cupid lent me his wings, and your sister Venus opened the casement.

MRS. SULLEN: I'm struck dumb with admiration!

ARCHER: And I — with wonder! *(Looks passionately at her.)*

MRS. SULLEN: What will become of me?

ARCHER: How beautiful she looks! — The teeming jolly spring smiles in her blooming face, and when she was conceived, her mother smelt to roses, looked on lilies — Lilies unfold their white, their fragrant charms. When the warm sun thus darts into their arms. *(Runs to her.)*

MRS. SULLEN: Ah! *(Shrieks.)*

ARCHER: 'Oons, madam, what d'ye mean? You'll raise the house.

MRS. SULLEN: Sir, I'll wake the dead before I bear this! — What! Approach me with the freedoms of a keeper! I'm glad on't; your impudence has cured me.

ARCHER: If this be impudence, *(Kneels.)* I leave to your partial self; no panting pilgrim, after a tedious, painful voyage, e'er bowed before his saint with more devotion.

MRS. SULLEN: *(Aside.)* Now, now, I'm ruined, if he kneels! — Rise, thou prostrate engineer; not all thy undermining skill shall reach my heart. — Rise, and know, I am a woman without my sex; I can love to all the tenderness of wishes, sighs, and tears — but go no farther. — Still, to convince you that I'm more than woman, I can speak my frailty, confess my weakness even for you — but —

ARCHER: For me! *(Going to lay hold on her.)*

MRS. SULLEN: Hold, Sir, build not upon that; for my most mortal hatred follows if you disobey what I command you now. — Leave me this minute. — *(Aside.)* If he denies, I'm lost.

ARCHER: Then you'll promise —

MRS. SULLEN: Anything another time.

ARCHER: When shall I come?

MRS. SULLEN: Tomorrow — when you will.

ARCHER: Your lips must seal the promise.

MRS. SULLEN: Pshaw!

ARCHER: They must! They must! *(Kisses her.)* — Raptures and paradise! — And why not now, my angel? The time, the place, silence, and secrecy, all conspire. And the now conscious stars have preordained this moment for my happiness.

(Takes her in his arms.)

MRS. SULLEN: You will not! Cannot, sure!

ARCHER: If the sun rides fast, and disappoints not mortals of tomorrow's dawn, this night shall crown my joys.

MRS. SULLEN: My sex's pride assist me!

ARCHER: My sex's strength help me!

MRS. SULLEN: You shall kill me first.

ARCHER: I'll die with you. *(Carrying her off.)*

MRS. SULLEN: Thieves! Thieves! Murder!

❖ ❖ ❖

The Transformed Peasant
by Ludvig Holberg (1723)
translated by Reginald Spink

JEPPE: a peasant
NILLE: his wife

> After finding Jeppe passed out drunk in a dunghill, a
> Baron takes him back to his house and, in jest, cleans him
> up as a gentleman and has his servants pretend that Jeppe
> is the Baron. Just as Jeppe gets used to the good life, they
> get him drunk again and return him to the dunghill. Now
> Jeppe must face his wife, Nille, who thinks he has gone to
> the market for soap, instead of spending the money on
> drink. Her stick, which she calls Master Eric, serves as
> punishment for Jeppe's ignorance.

> Suggested weapon: cane or staff

*A country scene in Denmark, outside a peasant's cottage.
Jeppe, in his peasant clothes again, is fast asleep on the
dunghill. Presently he wakes and, without looking up, calls
out:*

JEPPE: Hi, sekkertary, valet, lackeys! Another glass o' that
canary-bird!
*(Sitting up and gradually becoming conscious, he gazes
round him and rubs his eyes. He puts his hand to his head
and finds his peasant cap. He rubs his eyes again, turns the
hat over in his hands, and looks at his clothes. It is only
too clear that he is his old self again, and he gives vent to
a loud groan.)*
Oh!!! I knew it! I knew it! I'm myself again! I knew it was
too good to last! How long was Adam in Eden? The same
breeches, the same cuckoldy hat, the same — bed! Ugh!

No more canary-bird, no fancy glasses to drink out of, and no lackeys to stand behind my chair! I might have known it! Oh, oh, your lordship, you've come down in the world! Your bed's turned into a muck-heap and your lackeys are only pigs! There was I expecting to wake up and find rings on my fingers, and what's on 'em now? Faugh!! I wish I was back where I was before! I'll go to sleep again and see what happens.

(He lies down and presently is snoring heavily again. Nille appears from the cottage.)

NILLE: I wonder what can have happened to him. I hope he hasn't had an accident. More likely to be in some tavern drinking my money up! A fool I was to trust the drunken pig! Hullo, what's this? It's him, the villain! Fast asleep on the muck-heap! Fancy being married to that! I'll make you pay for this, you sot!

(She goes into the cottage to get her stick, and then stealing up to Jeppe she swipes him over the buttocks with it.)

JEPPE: Ow! Ow!! Help! Help!! What's that? Where am I? Who's that? What have I done? Ooh!!

NILLE: I'll teach you who it is, I will!

(She lets fly at him again, and finally pulls him by the hair.)

JEPPE: Don't, Nille! Nille, love, don't hit me anymore! You'll kill me! You've no idea where I've been!

NILLE: No, you drunken villain; that's just what I'd like to know! Where's that soft soap I sent you to get? Eh?

JEPPE: I haven't got any, Nille. I never got there.

NILLE: And why didn't you get there? That's what I want to know! Out with it! Where have you been?

JEPPE: Nille, I think I've been to Heaven.

NILLE: *(As she belabours him with the stick again.)* Heaven! Heaven, did you say? I'll Heaven you!! I'll teach you to come making jokes at my expense!!

JEPPE: Ow! Ow!! Ow!!! It's as true as I'm standing here, Nille!

NILLE: What's true?

JEPPE: That I've been in Heaven.

NILLE: You scoundrel, you! I'll give you Heaven!

JEPPE: Oh, Nille, dear, don't hit me!

NILLE: Then tell me where you've been, you wretch! Or I'll thrash you within an inch of your life!

JEPPE: Promise not to hit me, then, Nille.

NILLE: Out with it!

JEPPE: Promise not to hit me, Nille!

NILLE: I'll promise nothing!

JEPPE: As true as I'm standing here, Nille, I think I've been to Heaven. And I've seen things that'd surprise you. As sure as my name's Jeppe.

(Nille, giving him up as hopeless, drags him to the cottage, and opening the door, pushes him in.)

NILLE: There, you drunken pig! Stop there and sleep it off! And then we'll see about it! Heaven! Him!! Hell's more fit for the likes of him!!! Cock and bull stories!!! He'll get no more drink with money of mine! And if he gets anything to eat today or tomorrow he can think himself lucky. That'll teach him a lesson.

❖ ❖ ❖

Spring's Awakening
by Frank Wedekind (1891)
translated by Carl Mueller

WENDLA BERGMANN: a schoolgirl
MELCHIOR GABOR: a schoolboy

Awakening to their own sexuality, schoolmates Wendla and Melchior, who exist in the suffocating world between childhood and adulthood, meet in the forest and become aroused in each other's company. Their childlike curiosities turn to fixations and here their emotions get the better of them.

Suggested weapon: a switch or branch

A sunny afternoon. Wendla and Melchior meet by chance in the woods.

MELCHIOR: That you, Wendla? What're you doing up here all by yourself? — I walked in the forest for three hours and never met a soul, and suddenly you come along out of the trees.

WENDLA: It's me, Melchior.

MELCHIOR: If I didn't know you were Wendla Bergmann, I'd've taken you for a wood-sprite that fell from the trees.

WENDLA: It's only Wendla Bergmann. What are you doing here?

MELCHIOR: Thinking.

WENDLA: I'm looking for woodruff. Mother's making May wine. She was coming with me, but then Aunty Bauer came, and she doesn't like climbing, so I came by myself.

MELCHIOR: Found any woodruff?

WENDLA: A whole basketful. Over there under the beech trees

it's thick as clover. Right now I'm trying to find my way out. I guess I'm lost. What time is it?

MELCHIOR: Half-past three. — When do they expect you home?

WENDLA: Is that all it is? I lay down in the moss beside the brook and just dreamed for the longest time. Time passed so quickly I thought it must be evening already.

MELCHIOR: If they're not expecting you, let's sit down for a while. My favorite place is under the oak tree over there. Lean your head against the trunk and look up through the branches. It almost hypnotizes you. The ground's still warm from the morning sun. — I've wanted to ask you something for weeks now, Wendla.

WENDLA: I have to be home before five.

MELCHIOR: We'll go together. I'll carry the basket and we can strike out through the bushes and be at the bridge in ten minutes. The most amazing thoughts come to you when you lie here like this with your head propped in your hand.

(They both lie beneath the oak.)

WENDLA: What did you want to ask me, Melchior?

MELCHIOR: I've heard that you spend a lot of time visiting poor people. That you take them food and clothing, and even money. Why do you do that? Because you want to? Or does your mother tell you to.

WENDLA: Mostly because mother tells me. They're poor families with lots of children. And when the father can't find work, they freeze and go hungry. And we have so many things at home that we don't need. But how do you know about that?

MELCHIOR: Do you like going?

WENDLA: Oh, yes! You should know that without asking.

MELCHIOR: But the children are dirty, the women are sick, the houses filthy, and the husbands hate you because you don't have to work.

WENDLA: That's not true, Melchior. And even if it was, that's all the more reason to go.

MELCHIOR: What do you mean, all the more reason?

WENDLA: All the more reason to go. It makes me happy to help them.

MELCHIOR: You go to those poor people because it makes you *happy?*

WENDLA: I go to them because they're poor.

MELCHIOR: And if it didn't make you happy, you wouldn't go?

WENDLA: Is it *my* fault if it makes me happy?

MELCHIOR: And I suppose you think it'll get you into heaven! I've thought a lot about this for a long time now. Is it the miser's fault that visiting sick, dirty children doesn't make him happy?

WENDLA: Oh, but I'm sure it would give you the greatest happiness.

MELCHIOR: And so that's why the miser's condemned to hell! I'm going to write up an essay on that and give it to the Pastor. He's the one who started me thinking about it. He just loves the idea of *sacrifice!* And if he doesn't have an answer, I'll stop going to catechism class, and I won't be confirmed.

WENDLA: Why hurt your poor parents like that? Let them confirm you. They don't cut your head off. If only it wasn't for those awful white dresses of ours and the baggy pants *you* have to wear, we might even enjoy it.

MELCHIOR: There's no such thing as self-sacrifice! There's no such thing as selflessness! The good are happy and the bad are unhappy — and you, Wendla Bergmann, can shake your curls at me all you want! — What were you dreaming about earlier?

WENDLA: Just silly things — foolishness —

MELCHIOR: With your eyes open?

WENDLA: I dreamt I was a poor, poor little beggar girl who had to be out on the street by five every morning. And I had to beg all day long, whether it was rainy, or windy, or whatever. And I was always around rough, hard-hearted people. And when I came home at night, shivering with hunger and cold, I hadn't collected enough money to suit my father and he beat me — beat me —

MELCHIOR: You get those ideas out of crazy fairy-tale books. Brutal people like that don't exist anymore.

WENDLA: You're *wrong,* Melchior, they *do!* Martha Bessel gets a beating night after night so that the next day you can still see the *welts!* It makes me so furious I cry at night in my pillow. I've been thinking of how to help her for months now. I'll do *any*thing to change places with her for a *whole week.*

MELCHIOR: Somebody ought to report her father to the police. They'd take her away from him.

WENDLA: I've never been beaten in my life, Melchior. Not one time. I can't even imagine what it's like. I've hit myself, though, just to find out how it must feel, inside. It must be horrible.

MELCHIOR: I don't think it ever improved a child.

WENDLA: What?

MELCHIOR: Being beaten.

WENDLA: Like with this switch. Look how strong and slender it is.

MELCHIOR: A thing like that could draw blood.

WENDLA: Would you hit me with it once?

MELCHIOR: Who?

WENDLA: Me.

MELCHIOR: What's wrong with you, Wendla?

WENDLA: What difference does it make?

MELCHIOR: Be quiet! I'm not going to hit you!

WENDLA: Even if I say it's all right?

MELCHIOR: Don't be silly!

WENDLA: Not even if I begged you, Melchior?

MELCHIOR: Wendla! You're crazy!

WENDLA: I've never been beaten in my life!

MELCHIOR: How can you beg for a thing like that?

WENDLA: Please! Please!

MELCHIOR: I'll teach you how to say please! *(Beating her with the switch.)*

WENDLA: Oh, God! I don't feel it!

MELCHIOR: No wonder with all those skirts on!

WENDLA: Then beat my legs!

MELCHIOR: Wendla! *(Beating her harder.)*

WENDLA: You're not even *touching* me! Not even *touching!*

MELCHIOR: There! I'll show you! There! There! I'll show you! Bitch! Bitch!

(In a rage of passion, tears streaming down his face, Melchior throws aside the switch and begins beating Wendla with his fists. Suddenly he jumps to his feet, grasps his head in his hands, and runs sobbing into the forest.)

❖ ❖ ❖

Private Lives
by Noel Coward (1930)

ELYOT CHASE
AMANDA PRYNNE

> After divorcing years earlier, Elyot and Amanda meet up at a hotel while each is on their honeymoon with a new spouse. Their love for each other is rekindled, and they escape to Amanda's apartment in Paris, leaving each of their newlyweds, Victor and Sibyl, behind. In order to get along, they establish the word *Sollocks* as the calming factor when things begin to get vicious. However, the brewing violence, which defines Elyot and Amanda's relationship, spills over in this scene.

Suggested weapons: found

Amanda's apartment, Paris. Amanda goes to turn on the gramophone.

ELYOT: You'd better turn that off, I think.

AMANDA: *(Coldly.)* Why?

ELYOT: It's very late and it will annoy the people upstairs.

AMANDA: There aren't any people upstairs. It's a photographer's studio.

ELYOT: There are people downstairs, I suppose?

AMANDA: They're away in Tunis.

ELYOT: This is no time of the year for Tunis. *(He turns the gramophone off.)*

AMANDA: *(Icily.)* Turn it on again, please.

ELYOT: I'll do no such thing.

AMANDA: Very well, if you insist on being boorish and idiotic. *(She gets up and turns it on again.)*

ELYOT: Turn it off. It's driving me mad.

AMANDA: You're far too temperamental. Try to control yourself.

ELYOT: Turn it off.

AMANDA: I won't. *(Elyot rushes at the gramophone. Amanda tries to ward him off. They struggle silently for a moment, then the needle scratches across the record.)* There now, you've ruined the record. *(She takes it off and scrutinizes it.)*

ELYOT: Good job, too.

AMANDA: Disagreeable pig.

ELYOT: *(Suddenly stricken with remorse.)* Amanda darling, Sollocks.

AMANDA: *(Furiously.)* Sollocks yourself. *(She breaks the record over his head.)*

ELYOT: *(Staggering.)* You spiteful little beast.
(He slaps her face. She screams loudly and hurls herself sobbing with rage onto the sofa, with her face buried in the cushions.)

AMANDA: *(Wailing.)* Oh, oh, oh —

ELYOT: I'm sorry, I didn't mean it — I'm sorry, darling, I swear I didn't mean it.

AMANDA: Go away, go away, I hate you. *(Elyot kneels on the sofa and tries to pull her round to look at him.)*

ELYOT: Amanda — listen — listen —

AMANDA: *(Turning suddenly and fetching him a welt across the face.)* Listen indeed; I'm sick and tired of listening to you, you damned sadistic bully.

ELYOT: *(With great grandeur.)* Thank you.
(He stalks towards the door, in stately silence. Amanda throws a cushion at him, which misses him and knocks down a lamp and a vase on the side table. Elyot laughs falsely.)
A pretty display I must say.

AMANDA: *(Wildly.)* Stop laughing like that.

ELYOT: *(Continuing.)* Very amusing indeed.

AMANDA: *(Losing control.)* Stop — stop — stop —

(She rushes at him. He grabs her hands, and they sway about the room, until he manages to twist her round by the arms so that she faces him, closely, quivering with fury.)
I hate you — do you hear? You're conceited, and over-bearing, and utterly impossible!

ELYOT: *(Shouting her down.)* You're a vile-tempered loose-living wicked little beast, and I never want to see you again so long as I live.
(He flings her away from him. She staggers and falls against a chair. They stand gasping at one another in silence for a moment.)

AMANDA: *(Very quietly.)* This is the end, do you understand? The end, finally and forever.
(She goes to the door, which opens onto the landing, and wrenches it open. He rushes after her and clutches her wrist.)

ELYOT: You're not going like this.

AMANDA: Oh yes I am.

ELYOT: You're not.

AMANDA: I am; let go of me —
(He pulls her away from the door, and once more they struggle. This time a standard lamp crashes to the ground. Amanda, breathlessly, as they fight.)
You're a cruel fiend, and I hate and loathe you; thank God I've realized in time what you're really like; marry you again, never, never, never . . . I'd rather die in torment —

ELYOT: *(At the same time.)* Shut up; shut up. I wouldn't marry you again if you came crawling to me on your bended knees, you're a mean, evil-minded, little vampire — I hope to God I never set eyes on you again as long as I live —
(At this point in the proceedings, they trip over a piece of carpet and fall onto the floor, rolling over and over in paroxysms of rage. Victor and Sibyl enter quietly, through the open door, and stand staring at them in horror. Finally,

Amanda breaks free and half gets up. Elyot grabs her leg, and she falls against a table, knocking it completely over.)

AMANDA: *(Screaming.)* Beast; brute; swine; cad; beast; beast; brute; devil —

(She rushes back at Elyot, who is just rising to his feet, and gives him a stinging blow, which knocks him over again. She rushes blindly off left and slams the door, at the same moment that he jumps up and rushes off right, also slamming the door.)

❖ ❖ ❖

A Streetcar Named Desire
by Tennessee Williams (1947)

BLANCHE DUBOIS
STANLEY KOWALSKI

After staying with her sister, Stella, and brother-in-law, Stanley, it becomes apparent that Blanche's refinement does not mingle well with Stanley's unsophisticated existence. His suspicions of her lies are apparent after Stanley discovers that Blanche has been fired from her job as a schoolteacher because of her sexual exploits with younger men. Here, with Stella in the hospital about to give birth, Stanley has confronted Blanche with his findings. Sensing a confrontation, Blanche is on the phone desperately trying to get herself out of what she knows will be a dangerous situation.

Suggested weapon: broken bottle

Place, New Orleans.

BLANCHE: *(To Stanley.)* Don't come in here! Operator, operator! Give me long distance, please . . . I want to get in touch with Mr. Shep Huntleigh of Dallas. He's so well known he doesn't require any address. Just ask anybody who — Wait!! — No, I couldn't find it right now . . . Please understand, I — No! No, wait! . . . One moment! Someone is — Nothing! Hold on, please!
(She sets the phone down and crosses warily to the kitchen. Blanche presses her knuckles to her lips and returns slowly to the phone. She speaks in a hoarse whisper.)
Operator! Operator! Never mind long distance. Get Western Union. There isn't time to be — Western — Western Union!

(She waits anxiously.)

Western Union? Yes! I — want to — Take down this message! "In desperate, desperate circumstances! Help me! Caught in a trap. Caught in — " Oh!

(The bathroom door is thrown open, and Stanley comes out in the brilliant silk pyjamas. He grins at her as he knots the tasseled sash about his waist. She gasps and backs away from the phone. He stares at her for a count of ten. Then a clicking becomes audible from the telephone, steady and rasping.)

STANLEY: You left the phone off th' hook.

(He crosses to it deliberately and sets it back on the hook. After he has replaced it, he stares at her again, his mouth slowly curving into a grin, as he weaves between Blanche and the outer door.)

BLANCHE: *(Finally straightening.)* Let me — let me get by you!

STANLEY: Get by me! Sure. Go ahead. *(He moves back a pace in the doorway.)*

BLANCHE: You — you stand over there! *(She indicates a further position.)*

STANLEY: *(Grinning.)* You got plenty of room to walk by me now.

BLANCHE: Not with you there! But I've got to get out somehow!

STANLEY: You think I'll interfere with you? Ha-ha!

(She turns confusedly and makes a faint gesture. He takes a step toward her, biting his tongue, which protrudes between his lips.)

STANLEY: *(Softly.)* Come to think of it — maybe you wouldn't be bad to — interfere with . . . .

BLANCHE: *(Moving backward through the door into the bedroom.)* Stay back! Don't you come toward me another step or I'll —

STANLEY: What?

BLANCHE: Some awful thing will happen! It will!

STANLEY: What are you putting on now?

(They are now both inside the bedroom.)

BLANCHE: I warn you, don't I'm in danger!

(He takes another step. She smashes a bottle on the table and faces him, clutching the broken top.)

STANLEY: What did you do that for?

BLANCHE: So I could twist the broken end in your face!

STANLEY: I bet you would do that!

BLANCHE: I would! I will if you —

STANLEY: Oh! So you want some roughhouse! All right, let's have some rough-house!

(He springs toward her, overturning the table. She cries out and strikes at him with the bottle top, but he catches her wrist.)

Tiger — tiger! Drop the bottle top! Drop it! We've had this date with each other from the beginning!

(She moans. The bottle top falls. She sinks to her knees. He picks up her inert figure and carries her to the bed.)

❖ ❖ ❖

Extremities
by William Mastrosimone (1980)

MARJORIE
RAUL

> This is the opening of Mastrosimone's chilling play about power and control. Marjorie is alone in a house that she shares with two other women on the outskirts of town. It is morning, and she is lazily starting her day. She has just been stung by a wasp and has killed it when Raul arrives.

Suggested weapons: found

New Jersey, where the cornfield meets the highway. Marjorie's Kitchen. Enter Raul.

RAUL: Joe? Hey, Joe? It's me. O. How ya doin'? Joe in?
MARJORIE: *(Rising quickly, tying her robe.)* There's no Joe here.
RAUL: He said he'd be in.
MARJORIE: No Joe lives here.
RAUL: O.
MARJORIE: You always just walk in people's houses?
RAUL: O, I'm sorry. Excuse me. I'm really sorry.
MARJORIE: It's OK.
RAUL: Have a good day.
MARJORIE: You too.
RAUL: Thank you very much.
MARJORIE: You're welcome.
RAUL: You live here?
MARJORIE: Good guess.
RAUL: What, Joe move out?
MARJORIE: Joe who?
RAUL: Joe — I forget.
MARJORIE: There never was any Joe here.

RAUL: What's this, all one house, or apartments?

MARJORIE: All one house.

RAUL: He said he had a room here.

MARJORIE: Apparently he lied.

RAUL: Yeah, him or somebody else.

MARJORIE: I'm sorry, you have to go.

RAUL: Can I use the phone, please?

MARJORIE: No, I'm sorry.

RAUL: It's a local call.

MARJORIE: No, you have to go.

RAUL: *(Stroking the bicycle seat so gently.)* You ride a bike?

MARJORIE: No, I use it to collect dust. There's the door.

RAUL: I know where the door is. You don't have to tell me where the door is. This is a real bitch. The guy owes me alotta money. Said come pick it up.

MARJORIE: Well there's no Joe here.

RAUL: You sure, sweetheart?

MARJORIE: Maybe my husband knows. He's upstairs.

RAUL: Why don't you ask him, babe?

MARJORIE: He's busy right now.

RAUL: Busy.

MARJORIE: Sleeping.

RAUL: Sleeping.

MARJORIE: He's a cop.

RAUL: No kidding?

MARJORIE: And I have to wake him up in five minutes for work.

RAUL: Shh! You might wake him up.

MARJORIE: You better go now.

RAUL: Cop, eh? Go ask him if he knows a guy named Joe.

MARJORIE: I told you he's sleeping.

RAUL: I dropped Joe off at this house last week.

MARJORIE: I think you have the wrong house.

RAUL: No. This house. He's about six two. Rides a Triumph. Red beard. Wears cowboy boots. Short guy.

MARJORIE: There's no guy here.

RAUL: Except the cop.

MARJORIE: Honey, come down here please?

RAUL: Boy, that cop's a sound sleeper.

MARJORIE: Honey?

RAUL: What's amatter?

MARJORIE: Honey.

RAUL: Just like a cop: never there when ya need 'em.

MARJORIE: Honey!

RAUL: Honey! Honey! What's amatter wit him? Maybe he ain't here. Maybe you're tellin' me alittle lie eh, pretty momma? Maybe you think I scare easy. Go 'head. Go for the door. Let's see who's faster. So where's the other two chicks that live here?

MARJORIE: Kitchen.

RAUL: House full of people, and when you hollar, nobody comes. *(She bolts for the door; he cuts her off.)*

MARJORIE: Get out!

RAUL: You got a lousy bunch of friends.

MARJORIE: Get out right now!

RAUL: Take it easy, lovely. I saw the other two chicks leave this morning. The one wit' the ratty car should get here about five-thirty. The one wit specs, 'bout six. Today's gonna be a triple header.

MARJORIE: Get out!

(Long pause. Raul goes to door, looks at Marjorie, laughs, goes to phone, rips the wire out.)

RAUL: Your move.

MARJORIE: I'm expecting people anytime now. Anytime.

RAUL: No kidding? Dressed like that? Mind if I stick around for the fun? Your move.

MARJORIE: Don't touch me!

RAUL: Don't fight me. I don't want to hurt you. You're too sweet to hurt. Be nice. You smell pretty. Is that your smell or the perfume? Be nice. Wanna take a shower together first? I'll soap you up real good? Flip me alittle smile, babe.

I'm gonna fuck you frontways, backways, sideways, and ways you never heard of.

(She runs. He latches onto her hair, brings her down, mounts her, forces a pillow to her face. We hear her muffled screams.)

You gonna be nice?

MARJORIE: *(Muffled.)* Yes!

RAUL: You sure?

MARJORIE: *(Muffled.)* Yes!

RAUL: *(Removing the pillow slightly.)* Please don't wreck it. You made me hurt you, and I don't want to hurt you, but if you kick and scream and scratch, what else can I do, eh, babe? *(She tries to escape once more; he subdues her with pillow.)* That pisses me off!

MARJORIE: *(Muffled.)* Please!

RAUL: See what you made me do!

MARJORIE: *(Muffled.)* Please don't!

RAUL: Want me to put out your light?

MARJORIE: *(Muffled.)* No!

RAUL: You gonna be nice?

MARJORIE: *(Muffled.)* Yes!

RAUL: What's that?

MARJORIE: *(Muffled.)* Yes! Yes!

RAUL: Heh?

MARJORIE: *(Muffled.)* Please don't kill me!

RAUL: Can't hear you.

MARJORIE: *(Muffled.)* Please! Don't kill me!

RAUL: If you're nice! Be nice! *(Removing the pillow.)* You don't want me to do it again, eh? *(Shaking her head no.)* Maybe you like to get hurt, eh? *(Shaking her head no. Pause. He smothers her again out of whim. She goes limp.)* Holy mother of God. A freckle. I didn't know you had freckles. I love freckles. I want to kiss 'em all. Give 'em names and kiss 'em all good night. Yeah. The first time I saw you I knew it was gonna be beautiful, but I didn't think this beautiful. I didn't think anything could be this beautiful . . .

Not anything . . . Beautiful. *(He kisses her gently.)* Don't make your lips tight. They always make their lips tight. Do it nice. No. They're still tight. Kiss me nice. Yes. Yes. Nice. Smile. Smile! Nicer! How ya doin'? Answer me!

MARJORIE: What?

RAUL: How ya doin'? Say good.

MARJORIE: Good.

RAUL: Good. Invite me in.

MARJORIE: In where?

RAUL: Your house.

MARJORIE: We're already here.

RAUL: Nice place. Say thank you.

MARJORIE: Thank you.

RAUL: Kiss me and tell me you love me. Tell me!

MARJORIE: Please don't.

RAUL: Don't make it get ugly. Tell me you love me. Tell me!

MARJORIE: I love you.

RAUL: Say it nice.

MARJORIE: I love you.

RAUL: Tell me again and keep telling me.

MARJORIE: I love you I love you I love you . . .

RAUL: Yeah . . .

MARJORIE: I love you I love you I love you . . .

RAUL: More, more . . .

MARJORIE: I love you . . .

RAUL: How much?

MARJORIE: What?

RAUL: And what else?

MARJORIE: I love you.

RAUL: Yeah, and what else?

MARJORIE: Make love.

RAUL: Who?

MARJORIE: You.

RAUL: And who else?

MARJORIE: Me.

RAUL: You wanna make love?

MARJORIE: Yes.

RAUL: Say it.

MARJORIE: I want to make love.

RAUL: You say that beautiful. Again.

MARJORIE: I want to make love.

RAUL: When?

MARJORIE: I don't know.

RAUL: Now?

MARJORIE: I don't know.

RAUL: This is your last chance.

MARJORIE: I love you and I want to make love.

RAUL: Scream.

MARJORIE: What?

RAUL: *(He clamps her leg just above the knee and squeezes.)* Scream! Louder! More! See? Nobody hears. Just me and you, puta. Say you're my puta.

MARJORIE: Puta?

RAUL: Puta, puta, whore, my whore, my puta! Say it!

MARJORIE: I'm your puta.

RAUL: Say it and smile!

MARJORIE: I'm your puta.

RAUL: You like to tease me, eh, puta?

MARJORIE: No. Yes. Yes.

RAUL: You like to tease everybody.

MARJORIE: No.

RAUL: Know what you need, puta? You need acouple slashes here and here and here, stripes t' make you a zebra-face t'scare the shit outta anybody you go teasin', puta, cause you're mine, all mine. Say it!

MARJORIE: Yours!

RAUL: Undo the belt.

MARJORIE: Please! God!

RAUL: Undo it! This is gonna be beautiful, so you keep telling me, puta, and don't stop . . .

MARJORIE: I love you, I love you . . .

RAUL: You smell so pretty . . .

MARJORIE: I love you . . .

RAUL: You put perfume on for me?

MARJORIE: *(Seeing the aerosol almost in reach.)* Yes!

RAUL: Just for me!

MARJORIE: *(Reaching furtively, still too far.)* Yes! Yes! I love you! I love you!

RAUL: You say that more and more beautiful!

MARJORIE: *(In order to reach the aerosol, she must embrace Raul.)* I love you! I really really love you! I wanna be your puta!

RAUL: This is too beautiful!

MARJORIE: Yes!

RAUL: See! It don't have to be ugly, does it?

MARJORIE: No! No! Beautiful! I love you!

RAUL: I love when you hug me like that!

MARJORIE: I love you!

RAUL: Your perfume makes me drunk!

MARJORIE: I love you!

RAUL: You put it on for me?

MARJORIE: Yes!

RAUL: Just for me?

MARJORIE: *(Grabs the can.)* Just for you! *(Sprays his face. He screams, holds his eyes. Marjorie pushes Raul away with her foot and tries to run for the door but Raul latches onto her leg. Struggling to escape, she yanks an extension cord from the socket, loops it around his neck and pulls. He screams.)*

❖ ❖ ❖

Turandot
by Odyssey Theatre (1995)

PRINCE KALAF
GODDESS XI-WANG-MU

As the 999th suitor to Princess Turandot, Prince Kalaf has vowed to win the riddle competition, not to win her hand in marriage, but to avenge the death of his brother and those who blindly died for her beauty by losing their heads for answering wrong. With the help of the goddess Xi-Wang-Mu, he discovers that he truly loves the Princess and that he must choose his loyalties wisely.

Suggested weapon: sword or quarterstaff

Outside Peking. Kalaf enters, being drawn into the forest against his will by Xi-Wang-Mu.

KALAF: I will kill anyone who wished to detain me.
XI-WANG-MU: Ah! The mighty warrior. If you must fight, let us fight!
(They fight. At first Kalaf assumes he will win, but finds he is fighting someone who is equal or better.)
KALAF: Who are you?
XI-WANG-MU: She who does not like those who run away.
KALAF: I do not run away.
XI-WANG-MU: The love your brother offered you? Did you not run from that?
KALAF: He had to learn to stand alone.
XI-WANG-MU: What good did that do? It lost him his head.
KALAF: I promised to avenge him.
XI-WANG-MU: Then why are you not celebrating your triumph? You are the winner.

KALAF: How can I be a winner when the prize is not freely given?

XI-WANG-MU: You love her.

KALAF: I love them both!

(She has him on the ground by now, beaten. She magically makes images of his brother and Turandot to appear. She indicates them.)

XI-WANG-MU: Your life depends on which you choose. Your brother. Turandot.

(Kalaf looks at them both. They hold out their hands.)

KALAF: I love them both. I choose them both.

XI-WANG-MU: A wise choice, Prince. You will live.

(She takes the point away from his neck. The two images disappear. She looks at him. Leaves.)

KALAF: Yes. I love Turandot and I must find her. Turandot!

(Exit.)

❖ ❖ ❖

Scenes for Groups of
Three or More

❖ ❖ ❖

Roister Doister
by Nicholas Udall (c. 1540)

RALPH ROISTER DOISTER: a braggart
MATHEW MERYGREEKE: the fun-maker
DOBINET DOUGHTIE: a boy, servant to Roister
HARPAX: servant to Roister
CHRISTIAN CUSTANCE: a wealthy widow
MADGE MUMBLECRUST: an old woman, nurse to Custance
TOM TRUEPENNY: a boy, servant to Custance
TIBBET TALK-A-PACE: maid to Custance
ANNOT ALYFACE: maid to Custance

Mathew Merygreeke has been feeding Ralph Roister Doister's ego by encouraging him to woo the virtuous widow, Christian Custance, in exchange for food and drink. Despite the fact that Custance has already been promised to Gawyn Goodluck, Merygreeke assures Roister Doister of her affections. Custance wards off his advances, and Roister Doister's love soon turns to violence because of her humiliating refusals. He sets out to burn her home and kill her. Upon finding this out, Custance responds by waging a war against him with her servants.

Suggested weapons: household and kitchen items (tools, spades, and so on), quarterstaff or sword

London, outside Custance's house.

CUSTANCE: *(Rushing out.)* What caitiffs are those that so shake my house wall?
MERYGREEKE: Ah, sirrah! Now, Custance, if ye had so much wit,
   I would see you ask pardon, and yourselves submit.
CUSTANCE: Have I still this ado with a couple of fools?

MERYGREEKE: Hear ye what she saith?

CUSTANCE: Maidens, come forth with your tools!

(Enter the maids, armed and Truepenny with a drum and ensign.)

ROISTER: In array!

MERYGREEKE: Dubba-dub, sirrah!

ROISTER: In array!

They come suddenly on us!

MERYGREEKE: Dubbadub!

ROISTER: In array!

That ever I was born! We are taken tardy!

MERYGREEKE: Now, sirs, quite ourselves like tall men and hardy.

CUSTANCE: On afore, Truepenny!

Hold thine own, Annot!

On towards them Tibbet! For scape us they cannot.

Come forth Madge Mumblecrust! So! Stand fast together!

MERYGREEKE: God send us a fair day.

ROISTER: See, they march on hither!

TIBBET: But, mistress!

CUSTANCE: What sayst thou?

TIBBET: Shall I go fetch our goose?

CUSTANCE: What to do?

TIBBET: To yonder Captain I will turn her loose.

And she gape and hiss at him, as she doth at me,

I durst jeopardy my hand and she will make him flee.

(Custance and her forces advance to the fray.)

CUSTANCE: On! Forward!

ROISTER: They come!

MERYGREEKE: Stand!

ROISTER: Hold!

MERYGREEKE: Keep!

ROISTER: There!

MERYGREEKE: Strike!

ROISTER: Take heed!

CUSTANCE: Well said, Truepenny!

TRUEPENNY: Ah, whoresons!

CUSTANCE: Well done, indeed!

MERYGREEKE: Hold thine own, Harpax!

Down with them, Dobinet!

CUSTANCE: Now, Madge! There, Annot! Now stick them, Tibbet.

TIBBET: *(Singling out Dobinet.)*

All my chief quarrel is to this same little knave

That beguiled me last day. Nothing shall him save!

DOBINET: Down with this little quean that hath at me such spite!

Save you from her, master; it is a very sprite.

CUSTANCE: I myself will Monsieur Grand Captain undertake!

ROISTER: They win ground!

MERYGREEKE: Save yourself, sir, for God's sake!

(Merygreeke lands a blow on Roister's "helmet.")

ROISTER: Out! Alas, I am slain! Help!

MERYGREEKE: Save yourself!

ROISTER: Alas!

MERYGREEKE: Nay, then have at you Mistress!

(Pretending to strike at Custance he hits Roister.)

ROISTER: Thou hittest me, alas!

MERYGREEKE: I will strike at Custance here!

(Hits him again.)

ROISTER: Thou hittest me!

MERYGREEKE: So I will! Nay, Mistress Custance.

(Hits him again.)

ROISTER: Alas, thou hittest me still! Hold!

MERYGREEKE: Save yourself, sir. *(Hits him again.)*

ROISTER: Help! Out! Alas, I am slain!

MERYGREEKE: Truce! Hold your hands! Truce for a pissing while or twain!

(All cease fighting.)

Nay, how say you, Custance? For saving of your life,

Will ye yield, and grant to be this gentleman's wife?

CUSTANCE: Ye told me he loved me. Call ye this love?

MERYGREEKE: He loved a while, even like a turtledove.

CUSTANCE: Gay love, God save it, so soon hot, so soon cold!

MERYGREEKE: I am sorry for you. He could love you yet, so he could.

ROISTER: Nay, by Cocks precious, she shall be none of mine!

MERYGREEKE: Why so?

ROISTER: Come away. By the mat she is mankine
I durst adventure the loss of my right hand
If she did not slay her other husband.
And see, if she prepare not again to fight!

MERYGREEKE: What then? Saint George to borrow, our Lady's knight!

ROISTER: Slay else whom she will, by God, she shall not slay me!

MERYGREEKE: How then?

ROISTER: Rather than to be slain, I will flee.

CUSTANCE: To it again, my knightesses! Down with them all!
(The fight is resumed.)

ROISTER: Away! Away! Away! She will else kill us all!

MERYGREEKE: Nay, stick to it, like a hardy man and a tall.
(Hits him.)

ROISTER: Oh bones! Thou hittest me! Away! Or else die we shall!

MERYGREEKE: Away, for the pashe of our sweet Lord Jesus Christ!

CUSTANCE: Away, lout and lubber! Or I shall be thy priest!
(Roister flees followed by all his men.)
So this field is ours! We have driven them all away!

TIBBET: Thanks to God, mistress, ye have had a fair day!

CUSTANCE: Well, now go ye in, and make yourself some good cheer.

ALL: We go!

❖ ❖ ❖

Robin Hood and the Friar
anonymous (c. 1567)

ROBIN HOOD
LITTLE JOHN
FRIAR TUCK
MEN
LADY

> The spellings have been modernized in this Robin Hood play, included in its entirety. Although a number of characters come and go, it can also be modified to be used with only two people.

> Suggested weapons: quarterstaff or sword and buckler

> *A forest. Enter Robin Hood and his men.*

ROBIN HOOD: Now stand ye forth my merry men all,
And hark what I shall say;
Of an adventure I shall you tell,
The which befell this other day.
As I went by the highway,
With a stout frere I met,
And a quarter staff in his hand;
Lightly to me he leapt,
And still he bade me stand.
There were stripes two or three,
But I cannot tell who had the worse;
But well I knew the whoreson leapt within me,
And from me he took my purse.
Is there any of my merry men all
That to that frere will go,
And bring him to me forth withall,
Whether he will or no?

LITTLE JOHN: Yes, master, I make God a vow,
> To that frere will I go,
> And bring him to you,
> Whether he will or no.
> *(Exit Robin Hood and his men. Enter Friar Tuck with three dogs.)*

FRIAR TUCK: Deus hic! Deus hic! God be here!
> Is not this a holy word for a frere?
> God save all this company!
> But am not I a jolly friar?
> For I can shoot both far and near,
> And handle the sword and buckler,
> And this quarter staff also.
> If I meet with a gentleman or yeoman,
> I am not afraid to look upon him,
> Nor boldly with him to carp;
> If he speak any words to me,
> He shall have stripes two or three,
> That shall make his body smart.
> But, masters, to show you the matter
> Wherefore and why I am come hither,
> In faith, I will not spare,
> I am come to seek a good yeoman,
> In Barnisdale men say is his habitation.
> His name is Robin Hood,
> And if that he be better man than I,
> His servant will I be, and serve him truly;
> But if that I be better man than he,
> By my truth, my knave shall he be
> And lead these dogs all three.
> *(Enter Robin Hood seizing the Friar by the throat.)*

ROBIN HOOD: Yield thee, friar, in thy long coat!

FRIAR TUCK: I beshrew thy heart, knave, thou hurtest my throat.

ROBIN HOOD: I trust, friar, thou beginnest to dote:
> Who made thee so malapert and so bold
> To come into this forest here,

Among my fellow dear?

(Friar Tuck shakes off Robin Hood.)

FRIAR TUCK: Go louse thee, ragged knave.
If thou make many words,
I will give the on the ear,
Though I be but a poor friar.
To seek Robin Hood I am come here,
And to him my heart to break.

ROBIN HOOD: Thou lousy frere, what wouldst thou with him?
He never loved friar nor none of friar's kin.

FRIAR TUCK: Avant, ye ragged knave!
Or ye shall have on the skin.

ROBIN HOOD: Of all the men in the morning thou art the worst,
To meet with thee I have no lust;
For he that meeteth a frere or a fox in the morning,
To speed ill that day he standeth in jeopardy.
Therefore I had rather meet with the devil of hell,
Friar, I tell thee as I think,
Then meet with a friar or a fox
In a morning, or I drink.

FRIAR TUCK: Avant, thou ragged knave, this is but a mock!
If thou make many words, thou shall have a knock!

ROBIN HOOD: Hark, frere, what I say here;
Over this water thou shalt me bear;
The bridge is borne away.

FRIAR TUCK: To say nay I will not;
To let thee of thine oath it were great pity and sin;
But upon a friar's back and have even in.

ROBIN HOOD: Nay, have over

(Robin Hood climbs on Friar's back.)

FRIAR TUCK: Now am I, frere, within and thou Robin, without.
Now art thou, Robin, without, and I, frere, within,
To lay thee here I have no great doubt.

(Friar Tuck throws Robin Hood.)

Now am I, frere, without and thou, Robin, within!
Lie there, knave; chose whether thou wilt sink or swim.

ROBIN HOOD: Why, thou lousy frere, what hast thou done?

FRIAR TUCK: Mary, set a knave over the shone.

ROBIN HOOD: Therefore thou shalt abye.

FRIAR TUCK: Why, wilt thou fight a pluck?

ROBIN HOOD: And God send me good luck.

FRIAR TUCK: Than have a stroke for Friar Tuck.
(They fight.)

ROBIN HOOD: Hold thy hand friar and hear me speak!

FRIAR TUCK: Say on, ragged knave,
Me seemeth ye begin to sweat.

ROBIN HOOD: In this forest I have a hound,
I will not give him for a hundred pound:
Give me leave my horn to blow,
That my hound may know.

FRIAR TUCK: Blow on, ragged knave, without any doubt,
Until both thine eyes start out.
(Robin Hood blows his horn; his men enter.)
Here be a sort of ragged knaves come in,
Clothed all in Kendale green,
And to thee they take their way now.

ROBIN HOOD: Peradventure they do so.

FRIAR TUCK: I gave thee leave to blow at thy will;
Now give me leave to whistle my fill.

ROBIN HOOD: Whistle, frere, evil might thou fare!
Until both thine eyes stare.
(The Friar whistles; his men enter.)

FRIAR TUCK: Now Cut and Bause!
Bring forth the clubs and staves,
And down with those ragged knaves.
(They all fight.)

ROBIN HOOD: How sayest thou, frere, wilt thou be my man,
To do me the best service thou can?
Thou shalt have both gold and fee.
And also here is a lady free:
(Enter the Lady.)
I will give her unto thee,

And her chaplain I thee make
To serve her for my sake.
FRIAR TUCK: Here is a huckle duckle,
An inch above the buckle.
She is a trull of trust,
To serve a friar at his lust,
A pricker, a prancer, a tearer of sheets,
A wagger of ballockes when other men sleeps.
Go home, ye knaves, and lay crabs in the fire,
For my lady and I will dance in the mire,
For very pure joy.
(A dance.)

❖ ❖ ❖

Romeo and Juliet
by William Shakespeare (c.1594)
edited by Don Weingust

BENVOLIO
MERCUTIO
ROMEO
TYBALT
MEN

Mercutio and Benvolio, friend and member of the house of Montague, encounter Juliet's cousin Tybalt, of the rival house of Capulet. The Prince has decreed that any further public feuding will be punished by a sentence of death for the combatants. Romeo, a Montague, newly wed to the Capulet Juliet, attempts to make peace with Tybalt. Angered by Romeo's seeming cowardice, Mercutio goads Tybalt into fighting. As Romeo attempts to restrain his friend, Tybalt takes the opportunity to wound Mercutio mortally. Romeo's wish to make peace is now vanquished by his desire for revenge. At peril of his life, both in combat and from the Prince's edict, Romeo challenges Tybalt.

Suggested weapons: rapier, dagger

A street in Verona. Enter Mercutio, Benvolio, and men.

BENVOLIO: I pray thee good Mercutio let's retire,
   The day is hot, the Capulets abroad:
   And if we meet, we shall not 'scape a brawl, for now these hot days, is the mad blood stirring.
MERCUTIO: Thou art like one of these fellows, that when he enters the confines of a Tavern, claps me his Sword upon the Table, and says, God send me no need of thee: and by the

operation of the second cup, draws him on the Drawer, when indeed there is no need.

BENVOLIO: Am I like such a Fellow?

MERCUTIO: Come, come, thou art as hot a Jack in thy mood, as any in Italy: and as soon moved to be moody, and as soon moody to be mov'd.

BENVOLIO: And what too?

MERCUTIO: Nay, and there were two such, we should have none shortly, for one would kill the other: thou, why thou wilt quarrel with a man that hath a hair more, or a hair less in his beard, then thou hast: thou wilt quarrel with a man for cracking Nuts, having no other reason, but because thou hast hazel eyes: what eye, but such an eye, would spy out such a quarrel? thy head is as full of quarrels, as an egg is full of meat, and yet thy head hath been beaten as addle as an egg for quarreling: thou hast quarrel'd with a man for coughing in the street, because he hath wakened thy Dog that hath lain asleep in the Sun. Didst thou not fall out with a Tailor for wearing his new Doublet before Easter? with another, for tying his new shoes with old Ribbon, and yet thou wilt Tutor me from quarreling?

BENVOLIO: And I were so apt to quarrel as thou art, any man should buy the Fee-simple of my life, for an hour and a quarter.

MERCUTIO: The Fee-simple? O simple.

(Enter Tybalt, Petruchio, and others.)

BENVOLIO: By my head here comes the Capulets.

MERCUTIO: By my heel I care not.

TYBALT: Follow me close, for I will speak to them.

Gentlemen, Good den, a word with one of you.

MERCUTIO: And but one word with one of us? couple it with something, make it a word and a blow.

TYBALT: You shall find me apt enough to that sir, and you will give me occasion.

MERCUTIO: Could you not take some occasion without giving?

TYBALT: Mercutio thou consort'st with Romeo.

MERCUTIO: Consort? what dost thou make us Minstrels? and thou make Minstrels of us, look to hear nothing but discords: here's my fiddlestick, here's that shall make you dance. Zounds consort.

BENVOLIO: We talk here in the public haunt of men:
Either withdraw unto some private place,
Or reason coldly of your grievances:
Or else depart, here all eyes gaze on us.

MERCUTIO: Men's eyes were made to look, and let them gaze.
I will not budge for no man's pleasure I.
(Enter Romeo.)

TYBALT: Well peace be with you sir, here comes my man.

MERCUTIO: But I'll be hang'd sir if he wear your Livery.
Marry go before to field, he'll be your follower,
Your worship in that sense, may call him man.

TYBALT: Romeo, the love I bear thee, can afford
No better term then this: Thou art a Villain.

ROMEO: Tybalt, the reason that I have to love thee,
Doth much excuse the appertaining rage
To such a greeting: Villain am I none;
Therefore farewell, I see thou know'st me not.

TYBALT: Boy, this shall not excuse the injuries
That thou hast done me, therefore turn and draw.

ROMEO: I do protest I never injur'd thee,
But lov'd thee better then thou canst devise:
Till thou shalt know the reason of my love,
And so good Capulet, which name I tender
As dearly as my own, be satisfied.

MERCUTIO: O calm, dishonorable, vile submission:
Alla stucatho carries it away.
Tybalt, you Rat-catcher, will you walk?

TYBALT: What wouldst thou have with me?

MERCUTIO: Good King of Cats, nothing but one of your nine lives, that I mean to make bold withal, and as you shall use me hereafter dry beat the rest of the eight. Will you pluck your Sword out of his Pilcher by the ears? Make haste, lest mine be about your ears ere it be out.

TYBALT: I am for you.

ROMEO: Gentle Mercutio, put thy Rapier up.

MERCUTIO: Come sir, your Passado.

ROMEO: Draw Benvolio, beat down their weapons:
Gentlemen, for shame forbear this outrage,
Tybalt, Mercutio, the Prince expressly hath
Forbidden bandying in Verona streets.
Hold Tybalt, good Mercutio.
(Exit Tybalt.)

MERCUTIO: I am hurt.
A plague a both the Houses, I am sped:
Is he gone and hath nothing?

BENVOLIO: What art thou hurt?

MERCUTIO: Ay, ay, a scratch, a scratch, marry 'tis enough,
Where is my Page? go Villain fetch a Surgeon.

ROMEO: Courage man, the hurt cannot be much.

MERCUTIO: No: 'tis not so deep as a well, nor so wide as a Church door, but 'tis enough, 'twill serve: ask for me to-morrow, and you shall find me a grave man. I am pepper'd I warrant, for this world: a plague a both your houses. Zounds, a Dog, a Rat, a Mouse, a Cat to scratch a man to death: a Braggart, a Rogue, a Villain, that fights by the book of Arithmetic, why the dev'l came you between us? I was hurt under your arm.

ROMEO: I thought all for the best.

MERCUTIO: Help me into some house Benvolio,
Or I shall faint: a plague a both your houses.
They have made worms' meat of me,
I have it, and soundly, to your Houses.
(Exit.)

ROMEO: This Gentleman the Prince's near Ally,
My very Friend hath got his mortal hurt
In my behalf, my reputation stain'd
With Tybalt's slander, Tybalt that an hour

Hath been my Cousin: O Sweet Juliet,
Thy Beauty hath made me Effeminate,
And in my temper soft'ned Valour's steel.
(Enter Benvolio.)

BENVOLIO: O Romeo, Romeo, brave Mercutio is dead,
That Gallant spirit hath aspir'd the Clouds,
Which too untimely here did scorn the earth.

ROMEO: This day's black Fate, on moe days doth depend,
This but begins, the woe others must end.
(Enter Tybalt.)

BENVOLIO: Here comes the Furious Tybalt back again.

ROMEO: He gone in triumph, and Mercutio slain?
Away to heaven respective Lenity,
And fire and Fury, be my conduct now.
Now Tybalt take the Villain back again
That late thou gav'st me, for Mercutio's soul
Is but a little way above our heads,
Staying for thine to keep him company:
Either thou or I, or both, must go with him.

TYBALT: Thou wretched Boy that didst consort him here,
Shalt with him hence.

ROMEO: This shall determine that.
(They fight. Tybalt falls.)

BENVOLIO: Romeo, away be gone:
The Citizens are up, and Tybalt slain,
Stand not amaz'd, the Prince will Doom thee death
If thou art taken: hence, be gone, away.

ROMEO: O! I am Fortune's fool.

BENVOLIO: Why dost thou stay?
(Exit Romeo.)

❖ ❖ ❖

The Maid's Tragedy
by Francis Beaumont and John Fletcher (c. 1609)

ASPATIA: troth-plight wife-to-be of Amintor
AMINTOR: a noble gentleman
SERVANT

> After being forced to marry the king's mistress so that she can remain at court, Amintor has had to deny his true love for Aspatia. Not knowing this, Aspatia dresses as her brother, pretending to fight for her honor, but prepared to be killed if she cannot have the man whom she loves.

> Suggested weapons: rapier, dagger

Anteroom to Amintor's apartment. Enter Aspatia in man's apparel.

ASPATIA: This is my fatal hour, heaven may forgive
 My rash attempt that causelessly hath laid
 Griefs on me that will never let me rest,
 And put a woman's heart into my breast,
 It is more honour for you that I die,
 For she that can endure the misery
 That I have on me, and be patient too,
 May live and laugh at all that you can do.
 God save you Sir.
 (Enter Servant.)
SERVANT: And you Sir, what's your business?
ASPATIA: With you Sir now, to do me the fair office
 To help me to your Lord.
SERVANT: What, would you serve him?
ASPATIA: I'll do him any service, but, to haste,
 For my affairs are earnest, I desire

To speak with him.

SERVANT: Sir, because you are in such haste, would be loth to delay you longer: You cannot.

ASPATIA: It shall become you though to tell your Lord.

SERVANT: Sir he will speak with nobody, but in particular, I have in charge about no weighty matters.

ASPATIA: This is most strange: Art thou gold proof? There's for thee, help me to him.

SERVANT:. Pray be not angry Sir, I'll do my best.

(Servant exits.)

ASPATIA: How stubbornly this fellow answer'd me!
　　There is a wild dishonest trick in man,
　　More than in women. All the men I meet
　　Appear thus to me, are harsh and rude,
　　And have a subtlety in every thing,
　　Which love could never know; but we fond women
　　Harbour the easiest and the smoothest thoughts,
　　And think all shall go so. It is unjust
　　That men and women should be matched together.

(Enter Amintor and his Servant.)

AMINTOR: Where is he?

SERVANT: There my Lord.

AMINTOR: What would you, Sir?

ASPATIA: Please it your Lordship to command your man
　　Out of the room, I shall deliver things
　　Worthy your hearing.

AMINTOR: Leave us.

(Servant exits.)

ASPATIA: *(Aside.)* Oh, that that shape should bury falsehood in it.

AMINTOR: Now your will, Sir.

ASPATIA: When you know me, my Lord, you needs must guess
　　My business, and I am not hard to know;
　　For till the chance of war marked this smooth face
　　With these few blemishes, people would call me
　　My sister's picture, and her mine. In short,

I am the brother to the wrong'd Aspatia.

AMINTOR: The wrong'd Aspatia, would thou wert so too
Unto the wrong'd Amintor. Let me kiss
That hand of thine in honour that I bear
Unto the wrong'd Aspatia. Here I stand
That did it. Would he could not! Gentle youth
Leave me, for there is something in thy looks
That calls my sins in a most odious form
Into my mind, and I have grief enough
Without thy help.

ASPATIA: I would I could with credit!
Since I was twelve years old I had not seen
My sister till this hour I now arriv'd.
She sent for me to see her marriage,
A woeful one, but they that are above,
Have ends in everything. She used few words,
But yet enough to make me understand
The baseness of the injuries you did her.
That little training I have had, is war,
I may behave my self rudely in peace.
I would not, though, I shall not need to tell you,
I am but young, and would be loath to lose
Honour that is not easily gained again.
Fairly I mean to deal, the age is strict
For single combats, and we shall be stopped
If it be published. If you like your sword
Use it, if mine appear a better to you,
Change, for the ground is this, and this the time
To end our difference. *(Draws.)*

AMINTOR: Charitable youth,
If thou beist such, think not I will maintain
So strange a wrong, and for thy sister's sake,
Know, that I could not think that desperate thing
I durst not do. Yet to enjoy this world
I would not see her, for, beholding thee,
I am I know not what. If I have ought

That may content thee, take it, and be gone,
For death is not so terrible as thou,
Thine eyes shoot guilt into me.

ASPATIA: Thus she swore,
Thou wouldst behave thyself and give me words
That would fetch tears into my eyes, and so
Thou dost indeed, but yet she bade me watch,
Lest I were cousined, and be sure to fight
Ere I returned.

AMINTOR: That must not be with me,
For her I'll die directly, but against her
Will never hazard it.

ASPATIA: You must be urged,
I do not deal uncivilly with those
That dare to fight, but such a one as you
Must be used thus.
(She strikes him.)

AMINTOR: I prithee youth take heed,
Thy sister is a thing to me so much
Above mine honour, that I can endure
All this, good gods — a blow I can endure,
But stay not, least thou draw a timeless death
Upon thyself.

ASPATIA: Thou art some prating fellow,
One that has studied out a trick to talk
And move soft-hearted people, to be kicked.
(She kicks him.)
Thus to be kicked — *(Aside.)* why should he be so slow
In giving me my death.

AMINTOR: A man can bear
No more and keep his flesh. Forgive me then!
I would endure yet if I could. Now show
The spirit thou pretend'st, and understand
Thou hast no hour to live.
(They fight.)
What dost thou mean?

(He realizes that she cannot fight.)
Thou canst not fight! The blows thou makst at me
Are quite besides, and those I offer at thee,
Thou spreadst thine arms, and takst upon thine breast
Alas defenseless.

ASPATIA: I have got enough,
And my desire. There is no place so fit
For me to die as here.
(She falls.)

❖ ❖ ❖

Arden of Feversham
by George Lillo (1739)

BLACK WILL: ruffian
SHAKEBAG: ruffian
GREEN: enemy to Arden

Mosby, anxious to redeem the loss of his love Alicia to Arden, plots with his friend Green to have Arden killed. Two ruffians, Black Will and Shakebag, have been hired but have difficulty actually getting Arden to remain in one location to kill him. In this scene, they are arguing about who is more daring, when Green catches them being not so subtle about their hiding place.

Suggested weapon: rapier

A road or highway near Feversham.

SHAKEBAG: Damnation! Posted as you were, to let him escape!

BLACK WILL: I pray thee, peace.

SHAKEBAG: Green and I beheld him pass carelessly by within reach of your dagger. If you had held it but naked in your hand, he would have stabbed himself as he walked.

BLACK WILL: I had not power to do it; a sudden damp came over me; I never felt so in my life. A kind of palsy seized me.

SHAKEBAG: Palsy! When you're upon your duty! Go, go and sleep, or drink away your fears. You tremble still.

BLACK WILL: I tremble! My courage was never yet called in question, villain. When I fought at Boulogne, under the late king, both armies knew and feared me.

SHAKEBAG: That might be, because they did not know you. Dog, I'll shake you off to your old trade of filching in a throng — Murder's too genteel a business for your capacity.

— Sirrah, I have taken more gold at noon-day, than ever
you filched copper by candlelight.

BLACK WILL: Cowardly slave, you lie!

SHAKEBAG: A coward! S'blood! That shall be proved. Come on.

BLACK WILL: To thy heart's blood.

SHAKEBAG: To thine.

(They fight. Enter Green.)

GREEN: What are you mad! For shame! Put up your swords.

SHAKEBAG: Not till I've had his life.

BLACK WILL: Fool, guard thy own.

GREEN: Pray hear me, gentlemen!

BLACK WILL: Stand farther off!

SHAKEBAG: Away!

GREEN: This broil will ruin all.

SHAKEBAG: He begun it.

BLACK WILL: Ay, and will end it too.

GREEN: Arden, you know, returns, and will you let him escape
a second time?

SHAKEBAG: Who did the first?

GREEN: No matter, that may be repaired.

BLACK WILL: Brand me with cowardice!

GREEN: Come, come, you're both to blame.
Speak, will you lay aside this senseless broil?

BLACK WILL: Nay, let him speak.

SHAKEBAG: Why, rather than lose this opportunity—
(Puts up his sword.)

BLACK WILL: Ay — We'll defer it, 'till Arden's dead.
I'm for doing business first, and then for play.

SHAKEBAG: Challenge me when thou darest.

GREEN: The night draws on. Are you resolved?

SHAKEBAG: We are.

GREEN: Enough. — See where he comes. I must withdraw;
But when you've done the deed, and sent his soul
No matter where — I'll come to you again.
(Exit Green.)

BLACK WILL: Something rises in my throat — I can scarce

breathe — I'd rather poison half a dozen cardinals, than kill this honest man, but — I'll do't, for my reputation.

SHAKEBAG: He comes. Retire a little. Let him advance, then bury your dagger in his heart. If you fail, I'll second you.

BLACK WILL: Stand further off, I shall not need your aid.

SHAKEBAG: Now strike —

❖ ❖ ❖

Chrononhotonthologos
by Henry Carey (1782)

CHRONONHOTONTHOLOGOS: King of Queerumania
BOMBARDINION: his general
COOK
DOCTOR

In this nonsensical play, King Chrononhotonthologos, who cannot sleep, calls for a pageant and forbids the rest of his kingdom to rest while he cannot. Meanwhile, the King of the the Antipodeans has waged war on Queerumania, and Chrononhotonthologos leaves to fight alongside his general, Bombardinion. They are triumphant, but Queen Fadladinida, Chrononhotonthologos's wife, is actually in love with the now-imprisoned King of the Antipodeans. She confides this love to Cupid, who predicts that she will be a widow before nightfall. In this scene, the egotistical Chrononhotonthologos becomes offended when he is offered a plate of cold pork; Bombardinion responds.

Suggested weapon: rapier or whimsical weapon

Bombardinion's tent on the plains of Queerumania. Enter King and Bombardinion.

BOMBARDINION: This honour, royal sir, so royalizes
    The royalty of your most royal actions,
    The dumb can only utter forth their praise;
    For we who speak, want words to tell our meaning.
    Here, fill the goblets with Phalernian wine;
    And while our monarch drinks, bid the shrill trumpet
    Tell all the Gods that we propine their healths.
    (Trumpet sounds.)

KING: Hold, Bombardinion; I esteem it fit,
With so much wine, to eat a little bit.
BOMBARDINION: See that the table instantly be spread
With all that art or nature can produce:
Traverse from pole to pole; sail round the world;
Bring ev'ry eatable that can be eat;
The king shall eat, though all mankind be starv'd.
(Enter Cook.)
COOK: And it please your honour, there's some cold pork in the
pantry; I'll have it for his majesty in a minute.
(Cook exits in a hurry.)
KING: Hath'd pork! Shall Chrononhotonthologos
Be fed with swine's flesh, and at second hand?
Now, by the gods! Thou dost insult us, general.
BOMBARDINION: The gods can witness that I little thought
Your majesty to pork had such aversion!
KING: Away, thou traitor! Dost thou mock thy master?
(Strikes him.)
BOMBARDINION: A blow! Shall Bombardinion take a blow?
Blush, blush, thou sun! Start back, thou rapid ocean!
Hills, vales, seas, mountains, all, commixing, crumble,
And into chaos pulverize the world;
For Bombardinion has received a blow,
And Chrononhotonthologos shall die. *(Draws.)*
KING: What means this traitor? *(Draws.)*
BOMBARDINION: Traitor in thy teeth: Thus I defy thee.
(They fight; he kills the King.)
Ha! What have I done?
Go call a coach, and let a coach be call'd;
And let the man that calls it be the caller;
And in his calling, let him nothing call,
But coach, coach, coach! O for a coach, ye gods!
(Exits raving. Returns with a Doctor.)
BOMBARDINION: How fares your majesty?
DOCTOR: My Lord, he's dead.
BOMBARDINION: Ha, dead? Impossible. It cannot be!

I'd not believe it, though he himself would swear it.
Go join his body to his soul again,
Or by this hand thy soul shall quit thy body.
DOCTOR: My Lord, he's past the pow'r of physic;
His soul has left this world.
BOMBARDINION: Then go to the other world and fetch it back;
(Kills him.)
And if I find thou triflest with me there,
I'll chase thy shade through myriads of orbs,
And drive thee far beyond the verge of nature.
Ha! Call'st thou, Chrononhotonthologos?
I come! Your faithful Bombardinion comes!
He comes, in worlds unknown, to make new wars,
And gain thee empires num'rous as the stars.
(Kills himself.)

❖ ❖ ❖

The Musketeers
by Alexandre Dumas Père (1845)
translated by Frank J. Morlock

MORDAUNT
D'ARTAGNAN
PORTHOS
ARAMIS
ATHOS

The story picks up after the death of Richelieu; a stranger shows up at an inn and reveals that he, in the company of four other men, murdered the woman who seduced and ruined the stranger's brother, resulting in his death. The woman was actually Milady, Mordaunt's mother, and the other men were the Musketeers who Mordaunt now seeks to avenge her death. In this scene, the Musketeers have reunited and have found Mordaunt in an attempt to get to him before he succeeds in killing them. They explain that they would each like to fight him, but he argues that he cannot fight them all and should therefore be able to choose.

Suggested weapons: rapiers, cloak

The interior of the house of Cromwell — chamber shut by a door on the right.

D'ARTAGNAN: *(To Mordaunt.)* You have heard sir. The Comte de la Fere doesn't wish to have the honor of fighting with you. Choose among us which one will replace him.

MORDAUNT: Since I cannot fight with him, it doesn't matter to me with whom I fight. Put your names in a hat and I will draw by chance.

D'ARTAGNAN: There's an idea.

ARAMIS: In fact, this way's agreeable to all.

PORTHOS: I haven't thought of — now it's very simple.

D'ARTAGNAN: Let's see Aramis, write with the pretty little script you wrote to Marie Michon to warn her that the mother of this gentlemen wished to assassinate milord Buckingham.

(Aramis goes to Cromwell's bureau, tears three sheets of equal size, writes a name on each, then presents them to Mordaunt — who without reading them signals that he is in perfect agreement. Aramis rolls the papers, puts them in a hat, and presents them to Mordaunt, who draws one and lets the others fall with disdain.)

Ah, young serpent, I will sacrifice all my chance of promotion to Captain for that paper to carry my name.

ARAMIS: *(Reading the paper in a loud voice.)* D'Artagnan.

D'ARTAGNAN: Ah, there's still justice in heaven. *(Returning toward Mordaunt.)* I hope, sire, that you have no objection to doing it?

MORDAUNT: *(Drawing his sword and leaning on the point.)* None, sir.

D'ARTAGNAN: Are you ready, sir?

MORDAUNT: I am waiting for you, sir.

D'ARTAGNAN: Then take care of yourself, sir, I draw my sword often enough.

MORDAUNT: And I, too.

D'ARTAGNAN: So much the better! That puts my conscience at ease. En garde!

MORDAUNT: One moment. Give your word gentlemen, that you won't charge me all at once.

PORTHOS: Is it to have the pleasure of insulting us that you ask us this, sir?

MORDAUNT: No — it's to have, as the gentleman just said, an easy conscience.

D'ARTAGNAN: *(Looking around him.)* It must be for something else.

PORTHOS AND ARAMIS: Word of a gentleman.

MORDAUNT: In that case, gentlemen, place yourselves in some corner as the Comte de la Fere has done who doesn't wish to fight me but appears at least to know the rules of combat. And leave us space, we are going to need it.

ARAMIS: So be it.

PORTHOS: There's a lot of fuss.

D'ARTAGNAN: Arrange yourselves, gentlemen, there's no need to give the gentleman the least pretext for bad conduct. Come on, are you ready, sir?

MORDAUNT: I am.

(They cross swords.)

D'ARTAGNAN: Ah, you break away, you turn! As you like it — I will gain something — I won't see your nasty face — here I am now in the shadows. So much the better. You don't have any idea what a false look you have sir, when you are afraid. Look at my eyes and you will see a thing your mirror never shows you ever — that is to say a loyal and frank face.

(Mordaunt jumping back finds himself near a wall on which he leans with his left hand.)

Ah — now this time, don't break away anymore my fine friend. Gentlemen, have you ever seen a scorpion cling to a wall?

(At the moment when more relentless than ever, after a rapid and close feint, he hurls himself like lightning on Mordaunt, the wall seems to split. Mordaunt disappears through the gaping opening and the sword pressed between two panels breaks. D'Artagnan takes a step back. The wall shuts.)

Help, Gentlemen! Let's break this door.

ARAMIS: *(Running towards D'Artagnan.)* He's the demon incarnate.

PORTHOS: *(Pressing his shoulder against the secret door.)* He's escaping us, by God, he's escaping us!

ATHOS: *(Sourly.)* So much the better!

D'ARTAGNAN: I thought as much, by God! I thought as much — when the wretch turned around the room I foresaw some infamous maneuver. I knew that he contrived something but who could suspect this?

ARAMIS: It's a frightful misfortune that the devil, his friend, sends us.

ATHOS: It's a great good fortune, God sends us.

D'ARTAGNAN: In truth, you surrender Athos! How can you say such things to people like us! God's blood! You don't understand the situation? The wretch is going to send us a hundred ironsides. Who will grind us like grain in the mortar of Mr. Cromwell — Come on, come on, en route! If we remain even five minutes here, it's all over with us.

ATHOS AND ARAMIS: Yes, you are right. En route.

PORTHOS: And where are we going?

D'ARTAGNAN: To the hotel, take our clothes and our horses. Then from there, if it please, God, to France where at least I know the architecture of the houses. Our ship is waiting for us — my word it's still lucky — En route.

ALL: En route! En route!

❖ ❖ ❖

The Corsican Brothers
by Dion Boucicault (1852)

FABIEN DEI FRANCHI
CHÂTEAU-RENAUD
BARON DE MONTGIRON
ALFRED MEYNARD

> Angry at Louis dei Franchi for meddling in his affairs, Château-Renaud challenges him to a duel and kills him. A thousand miles away in Corsica, Louis's twin, Fabien dei Franchi, discovers that his brother has been murdered. He searches out his brother's murderer to kill him.

Suggested weapon: small sword

The forest of Fontainebleau. Mongiron and Renaud on stage as Fabien enters.

FABIEN: Stay!

MONTGIRON: What do I see?

RENAUD: *(In great terror.)* What would you?

FABIEN: Can you not guess?

RENAUD: Louis dei Franchi!

FABIEN: You take me for the spectre of your victim — no; I am one more terrible, more implacable. I am Fabien dei Franchi, come from the wilds of Corsica to demand of you where is my brother.

RENAUD: Of me? Of me? What have I to do with him?

FABIEN: You answer as the first murderer. Five days since, at the remotest end of Corsica, I learnt how I had lost a loved and only brother; how you drew your serpent slime across his path, blighted the bright vision of his days, tried to bring dishonour on a woman it was the devoted object of his life to guard. By a base lie you decoyed that woman into a snare from which he rescued her: then, taking advantage of a mere bravo's skill, you murdered him.

(Château-Renaud and Montgiron evince indignation.)

Yes — you are the assassin of my brother.

RENAUD: Assassin!

FABIEN: Ay, assassin. For when a man is deadly with his weapon and goads another less practiced than himself to quarrel, he fights him not, he murders him.

(Château-Renaud makes an action as if about to rush on Fabien.)

MONTGIRON: *(Interposing.)* Hold, hold! Gentlemen, I entreat you. Monsieur Fabien dei Franchi, I cannot comprehend you. Five days ago, you say you were in Corsica. How is it possible these sad details could have reached you in so short a space of time?

FABIEN: The dead travel quickly.

MONTGIRON: We are not children, sir, to be terrified with nursery tales.

FABIEN: On the same evening of my brother's death I was informed of all, *(Montgiron and Château-Renaud appear incredulous.)* nay more. I saw it all. *(A look of surprise and fear from Château-Renaud.)* In five days I have traversed two hundred and eighty leagues. When I reached your house, they told me you had just left Paris. I ascertained the route you had taken. I saw your carriage overturned and I exclaimed "The hand of the avenger is upon him."

RENAUD: *(Recovering himself.)* Well, sir, I am found. What would you with me?

FABIEN: A mortal combat. Know you not that the Corsican race is like the fabled Hydra — kill one, another supplies his place? You have shed my brother's blood — I am here to demand yours.

RENAUD: You wish to take my life! And how?

FABIEN: Not after the practice of my country, but in the manner sanctioned here, according to rule — according to fashion: you see I am in proper costume.

RENAUD: I would have avoided this most earnestly. I was flying from it. But if I accept the challenge, it is on one condition.

FABIEN: Name it.

RENAUD: That this quarrel ends here, and that I am not again to be called upon — let this be the *last* encounter.

FABIEN: The last it *shall* be. I am the only living relative of Louis, and after me, Monsieur de Château-Renaud, be assured none will trouble you.

RENAUD: Name your hour, place, and weapons.

FABIEN: The hour! I have sworn it should be at the moment when I met you. The weapons! With a sword you killed my brother, with a sword you shall encounter me. The place! The spot where we now stand.

RENAUD: *(Recoiling.)* This spot?

FABIEN: Yes, this spot; you chose it five days since. At the foot of that tree my brother fell; the traces of his blood remain there still.

RENAUD: Since you are determined, be it so.
(Takes off coat, vest, handkerchief, etc.)

MONTGIRON: Gentlemen, this cannot be. The duel is impossible; at least at present. Here is but one witness, and you are both unarmed.

FABIEN: You are mistaken, sir; I come prepared. Meynard, approach!
(Enter Alfred Meynard with two swords.)
Here is my second — here are arms for both.

MONTGIRON: Meynard, perhaps we may yet find means —

FABIEN: *(Taking off coat, etc.)* Monsieur Meynard, sir, knows his duty.

RENAUD: I am ready.

FABIEN: Meynard, request Monsieur de Château-Renaud to take his choice.
(Alfred presents the swords to Château-Renaud, who selects one, after trying the length, etc.)

RENAUD: Now sir. *(A distant clock strikes nine.)*

FABIEN: *(Very coolly.)* If you have any last instructions for your friend, you have still an opportunity.

RENAUD: Why should I use it?

FABIEN: Because, as surely as yon sky is now above us, in ten minutes you take your place there, where my brother fell.

RENAUD: This is no time for empty boasting, sir.

FABIEN: Come, sir — on guard!

(They fight for some moments. Château-Renaud exhausts himself in useless efforts.)

Pause for a moment, you are out of breath.

RENAUD: *(To Montgiron, sitting on trunk.)* His wrist is made of iron. *(To Fabien.)* When you are ready. *(In rising from the trunk of tree his sword catches against the ground and breaks.)*

MONTGIRON: Gentlemen — the sword of Monsieur de Château-Renaud is broken: The duel is over, the chances are no longer equal.

FABIEN: You are mistaken, sir. *(Breaks his sword.)* I have made them equal. Take up that fragment, and let us try once more.

MONTGIRON: Are you still implacable?

FABIEN: As destiny.

RENAUD: I shall fall, Montgiron; I feel sure of it. You will continue your journey alone. In eight days write to my mother, and say I had a fall from my horse. In a fortnight tell her I am dead. If she learned the fatal news abruptly, it would kill her.

MONTGIRON: Château-Renaud, you are mad.

RENAUD: No, but in ten minutes I am a dead man.

(Shakes hands with Montgiron.)

ALFRED: Are you ready?

(Château-Renaud and Fabien dei Franchi close in mortal conflict. Château-Renaud overthrows him; but just as he is going to strike, Fabien plunges his weapon into his breast. Château-Renaud falls into Montgiron's arms, who places him under the tree where Louis dei Franchi fell.)

FABIEN: Louis! Louis! I can weep for you now.

❖ ❖ ❖

The Web
by Eugene O'Neill (1913)

ROSE THOMAS: a dark-haired young woman looking thirty but really only twenty-two

STEVE: a cadet, he is a typical cadet, flashily dressed, rat-eyed, weak of mouth, undersized, and showing on his face the effects of drink and drugs

TIM MORGAN: a yeggman, he is short and thickset, with a bullet head, close-cropped black hair, a bull neck, and small blue eyes set close together

Steve has just returned home drunk to his wife and child, and obviously cares little for either of them. Rose, sick with consumption, tries to negotiate with him to take the night off from working, but he continues to bully her; even threatening to get rid of the baby when she tries to stand up to him. Tim, an old friend of Rose's, arrives on the scene just in time.

Suggested weapons: found, a gun

A squalid bedroom on the top floor of a rooming house on the lower east side, New York. Rose is having a coughing fit.

STEVE: *(His nerves shattered.)* Dammit! Stop that barkin'. It goes right trou me. Git some medicine for it, why don yuh?

ROSE: *(Wiping her lips with her handkerchief.)* I did but it ain't no good.

STEVE: Then git somethin' else. I told yuh months ago to go and see a doctor. Did yuh?

ROSE: *(Nervously, after a pause.)* No.

STEVE: Well den, yuh can't blame me. It's up to you.

ROSE: *(Speaking eagerly and beseechingly, almost in tears.)* Listen, Steve! Let me stay in tonight and go to the Doc's. I'm sick. (*Pointing to breast.*) I got pains here and it seems as if I was on fire inside. Sometimes I git dizzy and everythin' goes round and round. Anyway it's rainin' and my shoes are full of holes. There won't be no one out tonight, and even if there was they're all afraid of me on account of this cough. Gimme a couple of dollars and let me go to the Doc's and git some medicine. Please, Steve, for Gawd's sake! I'll make it up to yuh when I'm well. I'll be makin' lots of coin then and yuh kin have it all. (*Goes off into a paroxysm of coughing.*) I'm so sick!

STEVE: (*In indignant amazement.*) A couple of beans! What'd'yuh think I am — the mint?

ROSE: But yuh had lots of coin this mornin'. Didn't I give yuh all I had?

STEVE: (*Sullenly.*) Well, I ain't got it now, see? I got into a game at Tony's place and they cleaned me. I ain't got a nick. (*With sudden anger.*) And I wouldn't give it to yuh if I had it. D'yuh think I'm a simp to be gittin' yuh protection and keepin' the bulls from runnin' yuh in when all yuh do is to stick at home and play dead? If yuh want any coin git out and make it. That's all I got to say.

ROSE: (*Furiously.*) So that's all yuh got to say, is it? Well, I'll hand yuh a tip right here. I'm gittin' sick of givin' yuh my roll and gittin' nothin' but abuse in retoin. Yuh're half drunk now. And yuh been hittin' the pipe too; I kin tell by the way your eyes look. D'yuh think I'm goin' to stand for a guy that's always full of booze and hop? Not so yuh could notice it! There's too many others I kin get.

STEVE: (*His eyes narrow and his voice becomes loud and threatening.*) Can that chatter, d'yuh hear me? If yuh ever t'row me down — look out! I'll get yuh!

ROSE: (*In a frenzy.*) Get me? Wha'd I care? D'yuh think I'm so stuck on this life I wanta go on livin'? Kill me! Wha'd I care?

STEVE: (*Jumps up from the table and raises his hand as if to strike her. He shouts.)* Fur Chris' sake, shut up! *(The baby, awakened by the loud voices, commences to cry.)*

ROSE: *(Her anger gone in a flash.)* Sssshhh! There, we woke her up. Keep still, Steve. I'll go out, yuh needn't worry. Jest don't make so much noise, that's all.

(She goes over to the bed and cuddles the child. It soon falls asleep again. She begins to cough and rising to her feet walks away from the bed keeping her face turned away from the baby.)

STEVE: *(Who has been watching her with a malignant sneer.)* Yuh'll have to take that kid out of the bed. I gotta git some sleep.

ROSE: But, Steve, where'll I put her? There's no place else.

STEVE: On the floor — any place. Wha'd I care where yuh put it?

ROSE: *(Supplicatingly.)* Aw please, Steve! Be a good guy! She won't bother yuh none. She's fast asleep. Yuh got three-quarters of the bed to lie on. Let her stay there.

STEVE: Nix! Yuh heard what I said, didn't yuh? Git busy, then. Git her out of there.

ROSE: *(With cold fury.)* I won't do it.

STEVE: Yuh won't, eh? Den I will. *(He makes a move toward the bed.)*

ROSE: *(Standing between him and the bed in a resolute attitude, speaks slowly and threateningly.)* I've stood about enough from you. Don't yuh dare touch her or I'll —

STEVE: *(Blusteringly, a bit shaken in his coward soul, however.)* What'll yuh do? Don't try and bluff me. And now we're talkin' about it I wanta tell yuh that kid has got to go. I've stood fur it as long as I kin with its ballin' and whinin'. Yuh gotta git rid of it, that's all. Give it to some orphan asylum. They'll take good care of it. I know what I'm talkin' about 'cause I was brung up in one myself. *(With a sneer.)* What'd you want with a kid? *(Rose winces.)* A fine mother you are and dis is a swell dump to bring up a family in.

ROSE: Please, Steve for the love of Gawd lemme keep her! She's all I got to live for. If yuh take her away I'll die. I'll kill myself.

STEVE: *(Contemptuously.)* Dat's what they all say. But she's got to go. All yuh do now is fuss over dat kid, comin' home every ten minutes to see if it's hungry or somethin'! Dat's why we're broke all the time. I've stood fur it long enough.

ROSE: *(On her knees — weeping.)* Please, Steve, for Gawd's sake lemme keep her!

STEVE: *(Coldly.)* Stop dat blubberin'. It won't do no good. I give yuh a week. If yuh don't git dat brat outa here in a week den I will.

ROSE: Wha'd'yuh mean? What'll yuh do?

STEVE: I'll have yuh pinched and sent to the Island. The kid'll be took away from yuh then.

ROSE: *(In anguish.)* Yuh're jest tryin' to scare me, ain't yuh, Steve. They wouldn't do that, would they?

STEVE: Yuh'll soon know whether dey would or not.

ROSE: But yuh wouldn't have me pinched, would yuh, Steve? Yuh wouldn't do me dirt like that?

STEVE: I wouldn't, wouldn't I? Yuh jest wait and see!

ROSE: Aw, Steve, I always been good to you.

STEVE: Git dat kid outa here or I'll put yuh in the cooler as sure as hell!

ROSE: *(Maddened, rushing at him with outstretched hands.)* Yuh dirty dog!

(There is a struggle during which the table is overturned. Finally Steve frees himself and hits her in the face with his fist, knocking her down. At the same instant the door from the hallway is forced open, and Tim Morgan pushes his way in. Although distinctly a criminal type, his face is in part redeemed by its look of manliness. He is dressed in dark ill-fitting clothes and has an automatic revolver in his hand, which he keeps pointed at Steve.)

TIM: *(Pointing to the door, speaks to Steve with cold contempt.)* Git outa here, yuh lousy skunk, and stay out! *(As*

Steve's hand goes to his hip.) Take yer hand away from that gat or I'll fill yuh full of holes. *(Steve is cowed and obeys.)* Now git out and don't come back. If yuh bother this goil again I'll fix yuh and fix yuh right. D'yuh get me?

STEVE: *(Snarling and slinking toward door.)* Yuh think yuh're some smart, dontcha, buttin' in dis way on a guy? It ain't none of your business. She's my goil.

TIM: D'yuh think I'm goin' to stand by and let yuh beat her up jest 'cause she wants to keep her kid? D'yuh think I'm as low as you are, yuh dirty mutt? Git outa here before I croak yuh.

STEVE: *(Standing in the doorway and looking back.)* Yuh got the drop on me now; but I'll get yuh, yuh wait and see! *(To Rose.)* And you too!

(He goes out and can be heard descending the stairs. Rose hurries over to the door and tries to lock it, but the lock is shattered, so she puts the chair against it to keep it shut. She then goes over to the baby, who has been whimpering unnoticed during the quarrel, and soothes her to sleep again. Tim, looking embarrassed, puts the revolver back in his pocket and picking up the table sets it to rights again and sits on the edge of it. Rose looks up at him from the bed, half bewildered at seeing him still there. Then she breaks into convulsive sobbing.)

❖ ❖ ❖

The Women
by Clare Booth Luce (1936)

MARY
LUCY
SYLVIA
COUNTESS
MIRIAM

Set in the 1930s, a group of idle socialites spend their time gossiping about each other. Mary, a devoted wife who tries not to play into the game, has found out that her husband has been having an affair with Crystal, a seductive salesgirl looking to secure some of this fortune. Crystal succeeds in winning Mary's husband for her own, and at the advice of her friend, Sylvia, Mary heads to Reno for a divorce. Meanwhile, the Countess's gold-digging friend, Miriam, has been having an affair with Sylvia's husband. Sylvia then arranges for her own divorce and ends up at the same dude ranch where the ladies are staying. Here, she learns that her husband's affair was with Miriam, and a long-awaited confrontation between all of them ensues.

Suggested weapons: found

A ranch in Reno. Lucy enters left, takes Mary's hat.

MARY: Supper's nearly ready. As my last official act in Reno, I cooked the whole thing with my hands, didn't I Lucy?
LUCY: All but the steak and tomatoes and dessert, Mrs. Haines. *(Exits left.)*
MARY: *(Gives letter to Sylvia, glancing, as she does so, at inscription.)* For you Sylvia. From Edith?
SYLVIA: You couldn't miss that infantile scrawl. *(Pointedly.)* You didn't hear from anyone?

MARY: No.

SYLVIA: Well, darling, Stephen's hardly worth a broken heart.

MARY: The less you have to say about me and Stephen the better I like it!

SYLVIA: I'm only trying to cheer you up. That's more than you do for me.

MARY: I'm doing enough, just being pleasant to you.

SYLVIA: My, you have got the jitters, dear

MIRIAM: Hey, Sylvia, we're all out here in the same boat. Mary's laid off you. Why don't you lay off her?

SYLVIA: Oh, I'm just trying to make her see life isn't over just because Stephen let her down.
(Opens her letter. A batch of press clippings falls out. Countess picks them up, reads them idly, as Sylvia goes on with letter.)

COUNTESS: You see, Miriam? What else is there for a woman but l'amour?

MIRIAM: There's a little corn whiskey left. *(She pours another drink.)*

COUNTESS: Cynic, you don't believe in Cupid.

MIRIAM: That double-crossing little squirt! Give me Donald Duck. *(To Mary.)* Have a drink? *(Mary shakes head.)* Listen, Babe, why not relax? You'd feel better —

MARY: *(Laughing.)* Miriam, you're not very chatty about your own affairs.

COUNTESS: *(Suddenly engrossed by clippings from Sylvia's letter.)* Miriam, you sly puss, you never even breathed that you knew Sylvia's husband.

SYLVIA: *(Looking up from letter.)* What?

COUNTESS: Sylvia, listen to this from Winchell: "Miriam Vanities Aarons is being Renovated. Three guesses, Mrs. Fowler, for whose Ostermoor?" *(Sylvia snatches clippings from her.)*

MIRIAM: Why can't those lousy columnists leave a successful divorce alone?

COUNTESS: *(Reading another clipping.)* "Prominent stockbroker and ex-chorine to marry."

SYLVIA: *(To Miriam.)* Why, you dirty little hypocrite! *(During this, Peggy has entered and goes back of sofa. She listens but does not join group.)*

MARY: *(Going to her.)* Now, Sylvia —

SYLVIA: Did you know this?

MARY: No. But, Sylvia, why do you care? You don't love Howard —

SYLVIA: *(Brushing her aside.)* Love has nothing to do with it. She just wants Howard for his money!

MIRIAM: And what did you want him for? I made Howard pay for what he wants; you made him pay for what he doesn't want.

COUNTESS: Why Sylvia, I thought you said Howard was impotent? What a lovely surprise! Besides I'll stay bought. That's more than you did, Sylvia.

MIRIAM: If Howard's impotent, so is Ali Kahn.

SYLVIA: Why, you dirty little trollop!

MIRIAM: Don't start calling names, you Park Avenue pushover! *(Sylvia gives Miriam a terrific smack. In the twinkling of an eye, they are pulling hair. Mary seizes Sylvia's arm; Sylvia breaks loose. Countess tugs at Miriam's belt as Lucy comes in, looks at the fight with a rather professional eye, and exits for smelling salts.)*

COUNTESS: Girls, girls, calmez-vous! *(Her interference enables Sylvia to slap Miriam unimpeded.)*

MIRIAM: *(Shoving the Countess on the sofa.)* Out of the way, you fat old — ! *(Sylvia grabs Miriam's hair.)* Ouch, let go! *(Sylvia is about to use her nails. Mary takes a hand.)*

MARY: I won't have this, you hear! *(Mary's interference allows Miriam to give Sylvia a terrific kick in the shins.)*

SYLVIA: *(Routed, in sobs.)* Ouch! You bitch, you! *(As she turns away, Miriam gives her another well-placed kick, which straightens Sylvia up.)*

MIRIAM: Take that!

(Sylvia, shrieking with rage and humiliation, grabs Miriam again, sinks her white teeth into Miriam's arm. At this mayhem, Mary seizes her, shakes her violently, pushes her sobbing into the armchair.)

MARY: *(To Miriam.)* That's enough.

MIRIAM: She's drawn blood!

MARY: There's iodine in the bathroom.

MIRIAM: Iodine? I need a rabies shot. *(Exits right.)*

SYLVIA: *(Blubbering, nursing her wounds.)* Oh, Mary, how could you let her do that to me!

MARY: *(Coldly.)* I'm terribly sorry, Sylvia.

SYLVIA: The humiliation! You're on her side. After all I've done for you!

MARY: What have you done for me?

SYLVIA: I warned you!

MARY: *(Bitterly.)* I'm not exactly grateful for that.

SYLVIA: *(Hysterical.)* Oh, aren't you? Listen to me, you ball of conceit. You're not the object of pity you suppose. Plenty of the girls are tickled to death you got what was coming to you. You deserved to lose Stephen, the stupid way you acted. But I always stood up for you, like a loyal friend. What thanks do I get? You knew about that woman, and you stood by gloating, while she —

MARY: Get out of here!

❖ ❖ ❖

Running Dogs
by John Wexley (1938)

LIEUTENANT Li Pai Foo
PEASANT Tai Han
WU YEN: a soldier
LO SEE: a soldier

This pro-Communist play sympathetically depicts the struggles of the working class in China against the Imperial regime. Here, the peasant, Tai Han, proves to be the only individual who stands up for what he believes in, only to be beaten down for questioning the regime's blatant theft of crops from the peasant class.

Suggested weapon: club

The village of Chungsen, China. Lieutenant Li Pai Foo enters, followed by Wu Yen and Lo See. The Peasant cringes obsequiously before him.

LIEUTENANT: Who are you? What do you want? Speak up, I haven't all night to waste with you.

PEASANT: *(With his eyes downcast.)* I am the peasant, Tai Han, from the north of the village here. Today while I was in the fields, the soldiers of one of your companies came to my home and . . . and . . . there must be some grave error, your Excellency . . . some grave error indeed . . .

LIEUTENANT: *(Crossing to table, seats himself and lights a cigarette.)* What are you stammering? Hurry up! Don't speak in riddles.

PEASANT: Forgive me . . . I am not myself, I am so distraught But they came and took from me all my grain and rice for the winter. They beat my wife. I heard her scream but when I ran to my house, I saw them carrying away the baskets with grain. I ran after them and spoke with the sergeant . . . I implored him, I begged him . . .

(Lieutenant puffs his cigarette. Then removes his glasses and commences to polish them, studiously. We cannot be entirely sure that he is even listening to the Peasant.)

LIEUTENANT: Well, Well?

PEASANT: *(Perplexed.)* Possibly . . . forgive me . . . perhaps I have not made myself clear . . . but they took all my rice and grain . . .

LIEUTENANT: *(Pauses in polishing his glasses and barks sternly.)* We need grain. Our army requires food. Our soldiers cannot protect you from the bandits without being fed.

PEASANT: Of course. To be sure, but I . . . I must be paid for it, for my grain. It is all I have for the long winter. There is my woman and my aged father and four little ones. There are seven of us and we are expecting another one soon . . .

LIEUTENANT: *(Snaps suddenly.)* See here! Didn't the sergeant pay you?

PEASANT: *(Astounded.)* Why no! I knew you would see it, your Excellency. Perhaps he was drunk. He didn't pay me . . . he beat me instead and left me lying in the fields.

LIEUTENANT: *(Irritably.)* Which sergeant do you mean? Whom are you speaking of?

PEASANT: I do not know his name. But he is a thin man with a cast in one eye.

LIEUTENANT: Sergeant Po Yat, you mean, in charge of Company B. He reported to me that he paid for all of today's grain requisitions. You must be mistaken. *(He rises to leave.)*

PEASANT: *(Trembling, falls to his knees.)* That cannot be. No, he is mistaken. Please, forgive me, your Excellency. We will all starve if I am not paid or returned my rice and grain. We will all starve, your Excellency . . .

LIEUTENANT: *(Looking down on the crawling Peasant at his feet. With unconcealed disgust.)* You are a liar and a thief! You want to be paid twice. Get out of here, or I'll . . .

PEASANT: *(Pitifully.)* No, no. It is the truth!

LIEUTENANT: *(Shrugs.)* Then go to Sergeant Po Yat. Don't annoy me.

(He kicks the man off and starts to cross. The Peasant crawls after him, clutching the air wildly.)

PEASANT: *(Wailing.)* I cannot go to him again. He will beat me to death.

LIEUTENANT: *(Over his shoulder.)* I will too, in a minute. Now get out of here!

PEASANT: *(Rising. Then slowly.)* I have heard that the landlord here, Wan Fu, gets paid liberally for his grain. Only we, the peasants, are robbed.

LIEUTENANT: *(Wheeling. Angrily.)* What's that?

PEASANT: *(Sullenly.)* Yes, we are robbed and beaten. And then we are insulted and accused of being thieves ourselves. *(Suddenly crying out.)* It is true! All is true!

LIEUTENANT: Silence!

PEASANT: *(Hysterically.)* I will not keep silent. I cannot keep silent! You are thieves! Murderers! Rapists . . . !

LIEUTENANT: *(Strides over to him and slaps him hard across the mouth.)* Throw him out, the swine!

PEASANT: *(He is seized by Wu Yen and Lo See. He struggles with them.)* Yesterday one of your men raped my brother's child. Today she is dead — a corpse! Tomorrow we shall all be corpses!

(Lo See and the others beat him into silence and drag him to the exterior courtyard. The Lieutenant calls out to them.)

LIEUTENANT: Arrest him! Lock him up until morning. If he isn't quiet, I'll have his tongue torn out. Have the guard flog him twenty lashes, the thief! The lying thief!

(He exits into adjoining rooms. There is a moment of silence.)

❖ ❖ ❖

The Field
by John B. Keane (1965)

BULL MCCABE
TADHG MCCABE: Bull's son
BIRD: the town gossip
WILLIAM: an outsider

> Mrs. Butler, a widow, has put her field up for auction. Bull
> McCabe, who has tended the field as his own for years,
> arranges the bidding so that he will be the only buyer, pay-
> ing well below the asking price. However, William shows
> up to buy up the land for development. Here, Bull and his
> son Tadhg are waiting for William to scare him out of
> town before the auction. Bird is hovering nearby.

Suggested weapon: staff

*The west of Ireland. A gateway near the main Carraig-
thomond Road. Midnight.*

TADHG: Listen. *(He listens.)* It's bound to be him.
BULL: Who else could it be! . . . Pull back . . . He's coming near.
*(Bull and Tadhg withdraw into the shadows. Enter
William. He wears a light raincoat. Hearing a sound, he
stiffens and looks about him suspiciously. Bull emerges
from the shadows.)*
BULL: Turn around and go home!
WILLIAM: Who the hell do you think you are? I have as much
right to be here as you.
BULL: I'm telling you now for the last time . . . turn around and
go home!
*(William pauses, undecided. Bull flexes the ash plant in his
hand.)*
WILLIAM: I'm legally entitled to look at this field.

BULL: I want your solemn oath that you'll leave Carraig-thomond first thing in the morning and never set foot here again. Your solemn oath!

WILLIAM: Don't you threaten me!

BULL: You'll do as you're told or your wife won't know you when she sees you again . . . an' I'm not foolin' you, boy!

WILLIAM: For God's sake, get out of my way.

(He endeavors to advance, but Bull draws a sweeping blow with his ashplant, which William narrowly avoids.)

WILLIAM: Hey, that's dangerous!

BULL: Your solemn oath! Come on, your solemn oath that you'll quit Carraigthomond and never come back.

WILLIAM: Come on, have a bit of sense.

(He tries to advance again, but Bull repels him with the stick. Then Bull drops the stick.)

BULL: Come on! Pass us, if you're able!

(Behind him, silently, Tadhg emerges from the darkness.)

BULL: *(To William.)* Come on, if you fancy yourself.

WILLIAM: You won't goad me into assaulting you. A good night's sleep and you might see things a little clearer.

(William attempts to pass Bull, but Tadhg jumps on him from behind, hits him on back of head, and knocks him to ground.)

BULL: Hold on to him!

(Tadhg holds William's arms and Bull hits him heavily, skillfully, three or four times. William breaks from them, weakly desperate, but Tadhg grabs him by the legs and brings him to the ground again. Bull grabs his stick and beats William across the back and head. William's scream-ing dies out. Tadhg pulls William up as Bull stops beating him with his stick and gives William the knee. William falls helplessly. Bird rushes to Tadhg.)

BIRD: In the name of God, stop! . . . stop! . . . or you'll do for him.

(Tadhg throws Bird aside and gets in a crucial kick at William's head.)

BULL: Stop it! . . . Stop it! That's enough. We only want to frighten him.

TADHG: That's what he wanted, wasn't it?

BULL: *(Pulling him away.)* Now, if there's any questions about this, where were we tonight? What were we doing? . . . We were in the pub, the three of us. 'Tis ag'in the law but 'tis a sound excuse. Agreed? All to be on the one word. Come on now across the fields. That way we won't be seen . . . Move!

BIRD: You're after going too far. I don't like the look of him.

BULL: Get back to the pub! *(Bull pushes them off and turns to look down at William.)* Why couldn't you stay away, you foolish boy? Look at the trouble you drew on yourself, you headstrong foolish boy, with your wife and family depending on you . . . Jesus Christ —

(He kneels and examines William. He is suddenly aware that William is dead. He looks desperately around. Then rises and remains looking down at William. He then suddenly kneels and takes William's head in his lap and whispers an act of contrition. Looks around him and disappears into the night.)

❖ ❖ ❖

Hayavadana
by Girish Karnad (1972)

DEVADATTA: a slender, delicate-looking person, wearing a pale-colored mask
KAPILA: powerfully built and wears a dark mask
BHAGAVATA: the narrator
PADMINI: caught between Devadatta and Kapila

> Set in India, this philosophical tale posits the importance of intellect versus physique. Kapila, a physical wonder, and Devadatta, a poet, have both fallen in love with Padmini. Though betrothed to Devadatta, she is attracted to Kapila's energy and physique. When Devadatta realizes her affections for Kapila, he kills himself by chopping off his own head. Kapila finds him, and stricken with guilt, he follows suit. Padmini finds both of them and, in haste, replaces their heads on the wrong bodies. Kapila now has the body of a wrestler and a poet's mind, and Devadatta has a weak body and the mind of a wrestler. Padmini chooses Kapila, who has the best of both qualities, and Devadatta is rejected. In this scene, Devadatta confronts Kapila, but their bodies have changed once again. Having lived in the wild, Devadatta is now strong, and Kapila has become slender in domesticity. (At this point, the masks should be switched.)

> Suggested weapons: stylized sword, scimitar

> *Devadatta enters. He is holding a sword in one hand and in the other two dolls made of cloth.*

BHAGAVATA: Who! Devadatta?
DEVADATTA: Where does Kapila live here?
BHAGAVATA: Uhm — well — Anyway, how are . . . you . . .

DEVADATTA: If you don't want to tell me, don't. I can find out for myself.

BHAGAVATA: There. Behind those trees.

DEVADATTA: How long has Padmini been here?

BHAGAVATA: About four or five days.

DEVADATTA: Amazing! Even a man like me found the road hard. But how quickly she covers it — and with a child in her arms.

BHAGAVATA: Devadatta . . . *(Devadatta moves on.)*

There are only two words that make sense to Devadatta now — Kapila and Padmini! Kapila and Padmini! The words carry him along like a flood to the doorstep of Kapila's hut. But suddenly he stops. Until the moment he has been yearning to taste the blood of Kapila. But now he is still and calm.

(Kapila comes out.)

KAPILA: Come, Devadatta, I was waiting for you. I've been expecting you since yesterday. I have been coming out every half an hour to see if you'd arrived. Not from fear. Only eager.

(Padmini comes out and stands watching them.)

KAPILA: *(To Devadatta.)* You look exactly the same.

DEVADATTA: *(Laughs.)* You too.

KAPILA: *(Points to the sword.)* What's that?

DEVADATTA: *(Extending the hand that holds the dolls.)* Dolls. For the child. I came home from the fair. There was no one there. So I came here.

(Padmini steps forward and takes the dolls. But neither speaks. Padmini goes back to her place and stands clutching the dolls to her bosom.)

KAPILA: Come in and rest a while. There'll always be time to talk later. *(Devadatta shakes his head.)* Why? Are you angry?

DEVADATTA: Not any more. *(Pause.)* Did my body bother you too much?

KAPILA: It wasn't made for this life. It resisted. It also had its revenge.

DEVADATTA: Did it?

KAPILA: Do you remember how I once used to envy you your poetry, your ability to imagine things? For me the sky was sky, and the tree only a tree. Your body gave me new feelings, new words — I felt awake as I'd never before — even started — writing poems. Very bad ones, I'm afraid. *(They laugh.)* There were times when I hated it for what it gave me.

DEVADATTA: I wanted your power but not your wildness. You lived in hate — I in fear.

KAPILA: No, I was the one who was afraid.

DEVADATTA: What a good mix . . . No more tricks. *(They laugh.)* Tell me one thing. Do you really love Padmini?

KAPILA: Yes.

DEVADATTA: So do I.

KAPILA: I know.

(Silence.)

Devadatta, couldn't we all three live together — like the Pandavas and Draupadi?

DEVADATTA: What do you think?

(Silence. Padmini looks at them but doesn't say anything.)

KAPILA: *(Laughs.)* No, it can't be done.

DEVADATTA: That's why I brought this. *(Shows the sword.)* What won't end has to be cut.

KAPILA: I got your body — but not your wisdom.

DEVADATTA: Where's your sword then?

KAPILA: A moment.

(Goes in. Padmini stands looking at Devadatta. But he looks somewhere far away.)

BHAGAVATA: After sharing with Indra
his wine
his food
his jokes

I returned to the earth
and saw from far
a crack had appeared
in the earth's face exactly
like Indra's smile.
(Kapila returns with his sword. They take up positions.)
KAPILA: Are you still in practice?
DEVADATTA: Of course not. But you'd learned well. And you?
KAPILA: I learnt again. But one's older now . . . slower at learning.
DEVADATTA: *(Pause.)* You realize it's immaterial who's better with a sword now, don't you?
KAPILA: Yes, I do.
DEVADATTA: There's only one solution to this.
KAPILA: We must both die.
DEVADATTA: We must both die.
KAPILA: With what confidence we chopped off our heads in that temple! Now whose head — whose body — suicide or murder nothing's clear.
DEVADATTA: No grounds for friendship now. No question of mercy. We must fight like lions and kill like cobras.
KAPILA: Let our heads roll to the very hands which cut them in the temple of Kali!
(Music starts. The fight is stylized like a dance. Their swords don't touch. Even Padmini's reaction is like a dance.)
BHAGAVATA: *(Sings.)* Like cocks in a pit
we dance — he and I . . .
foot woven with foot
eye soldered to eye.
He knows and I know
all there's to be known
the witch's burning thirst
burns for blood alone.
Hence this frozen smile,
which cracks and drips to earth,
and claw-knives, digging flesh

for piecemeal death.

The *rishi* who said, "Knowledge gives rise to forgiveness" had no knowledge of death.

(Kapila wounds Devadatta who falls to his feet and fights. He stabs Kapila. Both fight on their knees, fall and die.)

❖ ❖ ❖

True West
by Sam Shepard (1980)

AUSTIN: early thirties
LEE: early forties
MOM: early sixties

> Austin, a screenwriter, has been living in his mother's home
> in California while she was vacationing in Alaska. His
> older brother, Lee, a thief and drifter, arrives and crashes
> Austin's meeting with a Hollywood producer to pitch an
> idea of his own. After much conflict and manipulation on
> both sides, Austin agrees to help Lee with the script. Here
> their mother has returned home to find her house in sham-
> bles after Austin and Lee have broken their truce.

> Suggested weapons: found

> *The kitchen. Lee sneers in Austin's face then turns to
> Mom.*

LEE: I'm gonna just borrow some a' your antiques, Mom. You
　don't mind do ya? Just a few plates and things. Silverware.
　*(Lee starts going through all the cupboards in kitchen,
　pulling out plates and stacking them on counter as Mom
　and Austin watch.)*
MOM: You don't have any utensils on the desert?
LEE: Nah, I'm fresh out.
AUSTIN: *(To Lee.)* What're you doing?
MOM: Well some of those are very old. Bone China.
LEE: I'm tired of eatin' outa my bare hands, ya know. It's not
　civilized.
AUSTIN: *(To Lee.)* What're you doing? We made a deal!
MOM: Couldn't you borrow the plastic ones instead? I have
　plenty of plastic ones.

LEE: *(As he stacks plates.)* It's not the same. Plastic's not the same at all. What I need is somethin' authentic. Somethin' to keep me in touch. It's easy to get outa touch out there. Don't, worry I'll get 'em back to ya.

(Austin rushes up to Lee, grabs him by the shoulders.)

AUSTIN: You can't just drop the whole thing, Lee!

(Lee turns, pushes Austin in the chest, knocking him backwards into the alcove. Mom watches numbly. Lee returns to collecting the plates, silverware, etc.)

MOM: You boys shouldn't fight in the house. Go outside and fight.

LEE: I'm not fightin'. I'm leavin'.

MOM: There's been enough damage done already.

LEE: *(His back to Austin and Mom, stacking dishes on counter.)* I'm clearin' outa here once and for all. All this town does is drive a man insane. Look what it's done to Austin there. I'm not lettin' that happen to me. Sell myself down the river. No sir. I'd rather be a hundred miles from nowhere than let that happen to me.

(During this Austin has picked up the ripped-out phone from the floor and wrapped the cord tightly around both his hands. He lunges at Lee, whose back is still to him, wraps the cord around Lee's neck, plants a foot in Lee's back, and pulls back on the cord, tightening it. Lee chokes desperately, can't speak and can't reach Austin with his arms. Austin keeps applying pressure on Lee's back with his foot, bending him into the sink. Mom watches.)

AUSTIN: *(Tightening cord.)* You're not goin' anywhere! You're not takin' anything with you. You're not takin' my car! You're not takin' the dishes! You're not takin' anything! You're stayin' right here!

MOM: You'll have to stop fighting in the house. There's plenty of room outside to fight. You've got the whole outdoors to fight in.

(Lee tries to tear himself away. He crashes across the stage like an enraged bull dragging Austin with him. He snorts

and bellows, but Austin hangs on and manages to keep clear of Lee's attempts to grab him. They crash into the table, to the floor. Lee is face down, thrashing wildly and choking. Austin pulls cord tighter, stands with one foot planted on Lee's back and the cord stretched taut.)

AUSTIN: *(Holding cord.)* Gimme back my keys, Lee! Take the keys out! Take 'em out!

(Lee desperately tries to dig in his pockets, searching for the car keys. Mom moves closer.)

MOM: *(Calmly to Austin.)* You're not killing him are you?

AUSTIN: I don't know. I don't know if I'm killing him. I'm stopping him. That's all. I'm just stopping him.

(Lee thrashes but Austin is relentless.)

MOM: You oughta let him breathe a little bit.

AUSTIN: Throw the keys out, Lee!

(Lee finally gets keys out and throws them on floor but out of Austin's reach. Austin keeps pressure on cord, pulling Lee's neck back. Lee gets one hand to the cord but can't relieve the pressure.)

Reach me those keys would ya', Mom.

MOM: *(Not moving.)* Why are you doing this to him?

AUSTIN: Reach me the keys!

MOM: Not until you stop choking him.

AUSTIN: I can't stop choking him! He'll kill me if I stop choking him!

MOM: He won't kill you. He's your brother.

AUSTIN: Just get me the keys would ya!

(Pause. Mom picks keys up off floor, hands them to Austin.)

AUSTIN: *(To Mom.)* Thanks.

MOM: Will you let him go now?

AUSTIN: I don't know. He's not gonna let me get outa here.

MOM: Well you can't kill him.

AUSTIN: I can kill him! I can easily kill him. Right now. Right here. All I gotta do is just tighten up. See? *(He tightens cord; Lee thrashes wildly. Austin releases pressure a little, maintaining control.)* Ya see that?

MOM: That's a savage thing to do.

AUSTIN: Yeah well don't tell me I can't kill him because I can. I can just twist. I can just keep twisting. *(Austin twists the cord tighter. Lee weakens, his breathing changes to a short rasp.)*

MOM: Austin!

(Austin relieves pressure. Lee breathes easier, but Austin keeps him under control.)

AUSTIN: *(Eyes on Lee, holding cord.)* I'm goin' to the desert. There's nothing stopping me. I'm going by myself to the desert.

(Mom moving toward her luggage.)

MOM: Well, I'm going to go check into a motel. I can't stand this anymore.

AUSTIN: Don't go yet!

(Mom pauses.)

MOM: I can't stay here. This is worse than being homeless.

AUSTIN: I'll get everything fixed up for you, Mom. I promise. Just stay for a while.

MOM: *(Picking up luggage.)* You're going to the desert.

AUSTIN: Just wait!

(Lee thrashes; Austin subdues him. Mom watches. holding luggage. Pause.)

MOM: It was the worst feeling being up there. In Alaska. Staring out a window. I never felt so desperate before. That's why when I saw that article on Picasso I thought —

AUSTIN: Stay here, Mom. This is where you live.

(She looks around the stage.)

MOM: I don't recognize it at all.

(She exits with luggage. Austin makes a move toward her, but Lee starts to struggle, and Austin subdues him again with cord. Pause.)

AUSTIN: *(Holding cord.)* Lee? I'll make ya a deal. You let me get outa here. Just let me get to my car. All right, Lee? Gimme a little head start and I'll turn you loose. Just gimme a little head start. All right?

(Lee makes no response. Austin slowly releases tension cord; still nothing from Lee.)

AUSTIN: Lee?

(Lee is motionless. Austin very slowly begins to stand, still keeping a tenuous hold on the cord and his eyes riveted to Lee for any sign of movement. Austin slowly drops the cord and stands. He stares down at Lee who appears to be dead.)

AUSTIN: *(Whispers.)* Lee?

(Pause. Austin considers, looks toward exit, back to Lee, then makes a small movement as if to leave. Instantly Lee is on his feet and moves toward exit, blocking Austin's escape. They square off to each other, keeping a distance between them. Pause. A single coyote heard in distance, lights fade softly into moonlight. The figures of the brothers now appear to be caught in a vast desertlike landscape. They are very still but watchful for the next move, lights go slowly to black as the afterimage of the brothers pulses in the dark. Coyote fades.)

❖ ❖ ❖

The Conduct of Life
by Maria Irene Fornes (1984)

ORLANDO: a lieutenant commander
LETICIA: his wife, ten years his elder
NENA: a destitute girl of twelve
OLIMPIA: a servant

> Orlando, a lieutenant commander who tortures political dissidents for the government, has been raping Nena while Leticia is away. Leticia, more of a mother to him than a wife, sensing Orlando's escalating violence, has been having an affair to get away from him. Here, he confronts her about it.

> Suggested weapons: found

> *A Latin American country, the present. Two chairs are placed side by side facing front in the center of the living room. Leticia sits on the right. Orlando stands on the down left corner. Nena sits to the left of the dining-room table facing front. She covers her face. Olimpia stands behind her, holding Nena and leaning her hand on her.*

ORLANDO: Talk.
LETICIA: I can't talk like this.
ORLANDO: Why not?
LETICIA: In front of everyone.
ORLANDO: Why not?
LETICIA: It is personal. I don't need the whole world to know.
ORLANDO: Why not?
LETICIA: Because it's private. My life is private.
ORLANDO: Are you ashamed?
LETICIA: Yes, I am ashamed!
ORLANDO: What of . . . ? What of . . . ? — I want you to tell us — about your lover.
LETICIA: I don't have a lover.

(He grabs her by the hair. Olimpia holds on to Nena and hides her face. Nena covers her face.)

ORLANDO: You have a lover.

LETICIA: That's a lie.

ORLANDO: *(Moving closer to her.)* It's not a lie. Come on tell us. *(He pulls her hair.)* What's his name? *(She emits a sound of pain. He pulls harder, leans toward her, and speaks in a low tone.)* What's his name?

LETICIA: Albertico.

ORLANDO: *(Takes a moment to release her.)* Tell us about it. *(There is silence. He pulls her hair.)*

LETICIA: All right.

ORLANDO: *(Releases her.)* What's his name?

LETICIA: Albertico.

ORLANDO: Go on. *(Pause.)* Sit up! *(She does.)* Albertico what?

LETICIA: Estevez. *(Orlando sits next to her.)*

ORLANDO: Go on. *(Silence.)* Where did you first meet him?

LETICIA: At . . . I . . .

ORLANDO: *(He grabs her by the hair.)* In my office.

LETICIA: Yes.

ORLANDO: Don't lie. — When?

LETICIA: You know when.

ORLANDO: When! *(Silence.)* How did you meet him?

LETICIA: You introduced him to me. *(He lets her go.)*

ORLANDO: What else? *(Silence.)* Who is he!

LETICIA: He's a lieutenant.

ORLANDO: *(He stands.)* When did you meet with him?

LETICIA: Last week.

ORLANDO: When!

LETICIA: Last week.

ORLANDO: When!

LETICIA: Last week. I said last week.

ORLANDO: Where did you meet him?

LETICIA: . . . In a house of rendezvous . . .

ORLANDO: How did you arrange it?

LETICIA: . . . I wrote to him . . . !

ORLANDO: Did he approach you?

LETICIA: No.

ORLANDO: Did he?

LETICIA: No.

ORLANDO: *(He grabs her hair again.)* He did! How!

LETICIA: *I* approached him.

ORLANDO: How!

LETICIA: *(Aggressively.)* I looked at him! I looked at him! *(He lets her go.)*

ORLANDO: When did you look at him?

LETICIA: Please stop . . . !

ORLANDO: Where! When!

LETICIA: In your office!

ORLANDO: When?

LETICIA: I asked him to meet me!

ORLANDO: What did he say?

LETICIA: *(Aggressively.)* He walked away! He walked away! I asked him to meet me.

ORLANDO: What was he like?

LETICIA: . . . Oh . . .

ORLANDO: Was he tender? Was he tender to you!

(She doesn't answer. He puts his hand inside her blouse. She lets out an excruciating scream. He lets her go and walks to the right of the dining room. She goes to the telephone table, opens the drawer, takes a gun, and shoots Orlando. Orlando falls dead. Nena runs to downstage of the table. Leticia is disconcerted, then puts the revolver in Nena's hand, hoping she will take the blame. Leticia steps away from her.)

LETICIA: Please . . .

(Nena is in a state of terror and numb acceptance. She looks at the gun. Then, up. The lights fade.)

Hot 'N' Throbbing
by Paula Vogel (1994)

WOMAN: Charlene, about thirty-four
MAN: Clyde, over thirty-four
BOY: Calvin, about fourteen

> After having a restraining order put on him for abusing his family, Clyde has returned to the house, drunk, expecting favors from his wife, Charlene. In defense, Charlene shoots at him, not to kill but to send him to the hospital by wounding him in the butt. After immobilizing him, they begin to reminisce, and Charlene gets caught up thinking of good times in their past. Their son, Calvin, who has been watching this from outside, tries to protect his mother from his father's charisma and potential violence.

Unarmed

Man and Woman on the sofa; the Boy stretched on the window. The Man starts unbuttoning the Woman's top.

WOMAN: What about your — ? — No, Wait —
MAN: Shh! Don't talk. Not now.
(The Man and Woman resume. Just then the door flies open violently; the Boy flies into the room.)
BOY: I AM. GONNA. KILL YOU!!
MAN: What the fuck — ?
(In a fury, the Boy throws himself on top of the couple. The Man and Boy roll on the floor. The Man screams.)
MAN: SHIT! AAAAH!
WOMAN: CALVIN! NO! STOP! Watch out for his butt!
(The Man and Boy wrestle. They stand. The Boy, from behind, gets the man in a lock, one hand pinned and twisted;

the Boy's arm is locked around the Man's throat, choking him.)

MAN: *(In a squeezed voice.)* It's getting harder to . . . be a . . . family man . . . these days.

BOY: You leave her alone. Understand?

WOMAN: Calvin. It's not. As it looks.

BOY: *You* don't live here anymore. Get it?

MAN: *(Appreciatively, in the same squeezed voice.)* You're getting . . . mighty big, son.
(And just as quickly, the Man slips around and out of the Boy's grip, quickly kneeing him in the groin. The Boy gasps and falls into a fetal position on the rug.)

WOMAN: Jesus Christ, Clyde!

MAN: He's playing with the big boys now.
(The Boy says nothing. His face, beet red, presses into the rug.)

WOMAN: Calvin —

MAN: Don't touch him. He'll be all right. *(Pause.)* Son? You all right? *(The Man offers his hand to the Boy, who refuses it and slowly gets up.)* I'm sorry. Reflex action. No man likes to injure the family jewels.

WOMAN: Calvin —

BOY: What's he doin' here?

WOMAN: Your father . . . just . . .

MAN: Dropped in. For a little adult conversation.

BOY: That's not what it looked like to me.

WOMAN: Honey, I can appreciate your concern, but he's still your father —

BOY: What's he doin' here? —

MAN: Look, maybe I should just call it a night.

WOMAN: No, wait a minute, Clyde. No matter what's happened between you and me, you and Calvin have to learn how to talk to one another. I will not be used as an excuse for getting in the middle of the two of you. Do you both hear me? I want you both to act civilized to each other in my living room for at least sixty seconds. *(Beat.)* I'm putting on a fresh pot of coffee.

(The Woman exits.)

MAN: Whatta night, huh?

(As the Man hobbles past the Boy to sit on the sofa.)

BOY: Hey, what happened to your butt?

MAN: Your poor, defenseless mother shot me.

BOY: Mom? Mom? She shot you?

(The Boy starts to laugh.)

MAN: I don't see anything particularly amusing about it. Men might hit you by the balls, but they do it to your face. Women — they shoot you in the butt.

BOY: You musta deserved it.

MAN: This is something private between your mother and me. *(Pause.)* So — how's school?

BOY: Okay.

MAN: And life? In general.

BOY: Okay.

(Another pause.)

MAN: Aren't you going to ask me how I'm doin'?

BOY: How are you, Dad?

MAN AND BOY: *(Together.)* I'm warmer than shit and tighter than mud!

❖ ❖ ❖

Skin
by Naomi Iizuka (1995)
an adaptation of Büchner's *Woyzeck*

POLICE 1
POLICE 2
JONES

> In this introduction to the character of Jones, we see the characters through Iizuka's expressionistic style of exaggeration and isolation. Much like Georg Büchner's *Woyzeck*, Jones has become alienated from the rest of society and must remain at the mercy of those above him. The location has been updated to an urban city, where police brutality is committed on anyone who looks suspicous.

> Suggested weapons: billy clubs

> *A man named Jones in the city in the night. Inside his brain is talk and static and classic rock and jamming Z90 and sweet sweet music from Baja California, Mexico. Then the Police slide out of the dark. Jones doesn't hear them. Jones doesn't see them. The Police are sly and invisible in their black and white machine. They have plastic faces the color of flesh. And they are America's finest and they say:*

POLICE 1: hey shithead
    hey punk
    hey motherfucker
    hold it — hold it right there —
POLICE 2: he said hold it punk —
POLICE 1: don't move —
POLICE 2: what are you —
POLICE 1: don't you fucking move —
POLICE 2: what are you — deaf —

POLICE 1: understand — do you understand —

POLICE 2: what is with this guy — you want to get smart — you want to be a smartass — boy — I'll fuck you up —

POLICE 1: watch it — punk —

POLICE 2: I will fuck you up —

POLICE 1: you need to listen up now — you need to settle down —

POLICE 2: settle the fuck down asshole —

POLICE 1: do you hear me — do you hear what it is I'm saying to you —

POLICE 2: you want to — you want to — I'll fuck you up — I will fuck you up —

POLICE 1: let's see some ID — we need to see some form of identification —

JONES: my name — you want to know — wait — you want to know my name — my name — hold on — I'm going to tell you — wait — my name — my name is superman — fucking superman —

(And here the dance begins. The Police proceed to beat him up.)

POLICE 1: superman —

POLICE 2: jones.

POLICE 1: this here is superman —

POLICE 2: jones. sean jones. 332-47-7106. 6/25/67.

POLICE 1: what's the matter with you, superman?

JONES: nothing.

POLICE 1: you sure about that?

JONES: yes sir.

POLICE 1: are you high, jones?

POLICE 2: he's asking you a question, shithead, what the fuck's the matter with you?

POLICE 1: are you high?

JONES: no, sir.

POLICE 1: I think you're high.

JONES: no, sir.

POLICE 1: I think you're flying, boy.

JONES: no, sir.

POLICE 2: let me see your eyes, superman —

POLICE 1: settle down —

POLICE 2: let me see your fucking eyes —

JONES: wait —

POLICE 1: I said settle down —

POLICE 2: LET ME SEE YOUR FUCKING EYES, SUPERMAN —

JONES: I CAN'T SEE —

(The dance ends. There is no other sound than the body, than the valves and arteries of the body. Jones bleeds. And his blood turns the whole world slowly gorgeous stinking red.)

POLICE 2: you're fucked up, you know that? you're a fucked up individual —

JONES: yes, sir.

POLICE 2: what were you doing back there?

JONES: nothing.

POLICE 2: I'm going to ask you again. what were you doing?

JONES: nothing.

POLICE 2: see, now, jones, that is an untruth. right now, see, I know you're lying to me.

JONES: no sir.

POLICE 2: I'm going to tell you what, jones, I see guys like you every night — I know you. I know what you are. I know every thought that goes through your head. I know every dream. I know what your story is. do you understand me?

JONES: yes sir.

POLICE 2: don't you ever lie to me — because if you lie, I will know. I will know because I know everything that happens here. you're bleeding, jones.

JONES: yes, sir.

POLICE 2: you're bleeding all over everything.

JONES: I'm bleeding.

POLICE 2: get out of here, jones. you're wasting my time. get lost. I said get out of here. disappear —

❖ ❖ ❖

The Lonesome West
by Martin McDonagh (1997)

COLEMAN CONNOR
VALENE CONNOR
FATHER WELSH

> After killing his father at point-blank range with a shot-gun, Coleman is being blackmailed by his brother, Valene, for the effects of their father's will. As Valene stakes claim to all household items, including the floor, the two brothers continually argue about stoves, poteen, Valene's collection of saint figurines, and crisps.

> Suggested weapons: found

A kitchen in Leenane in the west of Ireland. Valene takes his poteen out of his biscuit tin to check if any is missing. Coleman puts his magazine aside, takes his glasses off, and sits at the table.

VALENE: You've been at this.

COLEMAN: I haven't at all been at that.

VALENE: It seems very . . . reduced.

COLEMAN: Reduced me arse. I wouldn't be at yours if you shoved a fecking . . .

VALENE: *(Sipping it, uncertain.)* You've topped it up with water.

COLEMAN: Be believing what you wish. I never touched your poteen.

VALENE: Where would you get money for . . . Me house insurance?! Oh you fecker . . . !
(Valene desperately finds and examines his insurance book.)

COLEMAN: I paid in your house insurance.

VALENE: This isn't Duffy's signature.

COLEMAN: It is Duffy's signature. Doesn't it say "Duffy"?

VALENE: You paid it?

COLEMAN: Aye.

VALENE: Why?

COLEMAN: Oh to do you a favour, after all the favours you've done me over the years. Oh aye.

VALENE: It's easy enough to check.

COLEMAN: It is easy enough to check, and check ahead, ya feck. Check until you're blue in the face.

(Confused, Valene puts the book away.)

It's not only money can buy you booze. No. Sex appeal it is too.

VALENE: Sex appeal? You? Your sex appeal wouldn't buy the phlegm off a dead frog.

COLEMAN: You have your own opinion and you're well entitled to it. Girleen's of the opposite opinion.

VALENE: Girleen? Me arse.

COLEMAN: Is true.

VALENE: Eh?

COLEMAN: I said let me have a bottle on tick and I'll be giving you a big kiss, now. She said "If you let me be touching you below, sure you can have a bottle for nothing." The deal was struck then and there.

VALENE: Girleen wouldn't touch you below if you bought her a pony, let alone giving poteen away on top of it.

COLEMAN: I can only be telling the God's honest truth, and how else would I be getting poteen for free?

VALENE: *(Unsure.)* Me arse. *(Pause.)* Eh? *(Pause.)* Girleen's pretty. *(Pause.)* Girleen's awful pretty. *(Pause.)* Why would Girleen be touching you below?

COLEMAN: Mature men it is Girleen likes.

VALENE: I don't believe you at all.

COLEMAN: Don't so.

VALENE: *(Pause.)* What did it feel like?

COLEMAN: What did what feel like?

VALENE: The touching below.

COLEMAN: Em, nice enough now.

VALENE: *(Unsure.)* I don't believe you at all. *(Pause.)* No, I don't believe you at all.

(Coleman opens and starts eating a packet of Valene's crisps.)

Girleen wouldn't be touching you below. Never in the world would Girleen be touching y . . . *(Stunned.)* Who said you could go eating me crisps?!

COLEMAN: Nobody said.

VALENE: In front of me?!

COLEMAN: I decided of me own accord.

VALENE: You'll be paying me seventeen pee of your own accord so! And right now you'll be paying me!

COLEMAN: Right now, is it?

VALENE: It is!

COLEMAN: The money you have stashed?

VALENE: And if you don't pay up it's a batter I'll be giving you.

COLEMAN: A batter from you? I'd be as scared of a batter from a worm.

VALENE: Seventeen pee I'm saying!

(Pause. Coleman slowly takes a coin out of his pocket and, without looking at it, slams it down on the table. Valene looks at the coin.)

That's ten.

(Coleman looks at the coin, takes out another one and slams that down also.)

COLEMAN: You can keep the change.

VALENE: I can keep the change, can I?

(He pockets the coins, takes out three pee, opens one of Coleman's hands and places the money in it.)

I'm in no need of charity.

(He turns away. Still sitting, Coleman throws the coins hard at the back of Valene's head.)

Ya fecker ya!! Come on so!

(Coleman jumps up, knocking his chair over.)

COLEMAN: Come on so, is it?

VALENE: Pegging good money at me?!

COLEMAN: It is. And be picking that money up now, for your oul piggy-bank, ya little virgin fecking gayboy ya . . .

(*The two grapple, fall to the floor, and roll around scuffling. Welsh enters through the front door, slightly drunk.*)

WELSH: Hey ye's two! Ye's two! (*Pause. Loudly.*) Ye's two!

COLEMAN: (*Irritated.*) Wha?

WELSH: Tom Hanlon's just killed himself.

VALENE: Eh?

WELSH: Tom Hanlon's just killed himself.

VALENE: (*Pause.*) Let go o' me neck, you.

COLEMAN: Let go o' me arm so.

(*The two slowly let go of each other and stand up, as Welsh sits at the table, stunned.*

❖ ❖ ❖

Glossary

abye   to endure (page 97).

addle   to spoil (page 100).

alla stucatho   a thrust in fencing, also; *stucaddo* (page 100).

array   to prepare for battle (page 91).

ballockes   testicles (page 98).

bause   to exclaim, shout (page 97).

by the way   at the field where they will fight (page 12).

buckle   to grapple, engage with an adversary (page 51).

caitiffs   a contemptible wretch (page 90).

carp   to contend with (page 95).

catchpoll   Sheriff's officer (page 58).

crabs   crabapples (page 98).

despight   contempt (page 54).

frawer   a tapster at a tavern, someone who pours the drinks (page 100).

fee-simple   an estate, belonging to the owner and his heirs unconditionally (page 100).

frieze jerkin   a close-fitting jacket, jersey, or short coat, made of a kind of coarse woolen cloth (page 58).

gat   a revolver, handgun (page 127).

good den   a salutation like good evening, but can be used at any time after noon (page 100).

keisar   Emperor (page 55).

loth   hateful (page 105).

lucifer box   a match box (page 22).

hilding   a contemptible woman (page 35).

mankine   infuriated (page 93).

maugre   in spite of (page 53).

mire   a piece of wet ground (page 98).

moly   a mythical herb with a white flower and black root and endowed with magic properties (page 3).

narky   sarcastic (page 27).

parley   to request a conference with an enemy to discuss the terms of a dispute (page 53).

pashe   passion, in the religious sense (page 93).

passado   a forward thrust with the sword (page 102).

pilcher   a scabbard (page 102).

quean   a bold, impudent, or ill-behaved woman (page 92).

saveguard   an outer petticoat worn by women to protect their dress when riding (page 58).

sect   sex (page 56).

stave   a stick (page 97).

stripe   a blow or stroke with a staff or other weapon (page 94).

trow   to trust, believe (page 56).

trull   a girl, lass, or wench (page 98).

untruss a point   to unfasten a point of metal at the end of a lace, also known as a tag; used to assist its insertion through an eyelet hole on clothing that is laced up. There is a play on the words in Moll's next line to Laxton, regarding her weapon (page 59).

woodruff   a sweet-scented herb (page 68).

yeoman   a commoner or countryman of respectable standing (page 95).

yeggman   a burglar or safe breaker (page 123).

Permission Acknowledgments

About the Editors

KYNA HAMILL (M.A., University of Alberta) is currently completing her Ph.D. dissertation at Tufts University. She is a certified member of Fight Directors Canada and a recognized member of the International Order of the Sword and the Pen. Her research areas include violence as entertainment, contemporary Irish theater, the Italian commedia dell'arte, and the history of staged combat.

DON WEINGUST (Ph.D., University of California at Berkeley) is an assistant professor and member of the graduate faculty in the Department of Drama and Dance at Tufts University. Specializing in Shakespearean text and performance, he teaches courses in Dramatic Literature, History, and Theory and Criticism. A director, professional actor, and member of Actors Equity Association, he has worked Off-Broadway and with major regional repertory theaters.